The Mirror Diary

Garrett Hongo

The Mirror Diary

SELECTED ESSAYS

UNIVERSITY OF MICHIGAN PRESS

Ann Arbor

Published in the United States of America by the
University of Michigan Press
Manufactured in the United States of America
♾ Printed on acid-free paper

2020   2019   2018   2017   4   3   2   1

A CIP catalog record for this book is available from the British Library.

Library of Congress Cataloging-in-Publication data has been applied for.

ISBN 978–0–472–03702–5 (paper : alk. paper)
ISBN 978–0–472–12329–2 (e-book)

To the memory of Bert Meyers
(1928–1979)

Some men were words that warmed a room.

Acknowledgments

I'd like to thank the editors of the periodicals, anthologies, and other books in which these writings, some in slightly different versions, first appeared:

"The Activity of the Poet." *Ohio Review* 41 (Summer 1988): 75–92.

"America Singing: An Address to the Newly Arrived Peoples." *Parnassus: Poetry in Review* 17, no. 1 (1992): 9–20.

"Gardens We Have Left: Against Nationalisms in Literature." *Profession* (1997): 18–22.

"Garrett Hongo: A Poet's Notebook." In *The Poet's Notebook*, edited by Stephen Kuusisto, Deborah Tall, and David Weiss, 102–9. New York: Norton, 1995.

"Homage to Lost Worlds: Where I Write, Why I Write There." *Rivendell: City of Angels.* 2002.

"Hope Alive: Writers at the Unconvention." *LA Weekly,* September 6–13, 1996, 9–10.

"HR 442: Redress." In *Outside the Law: Narratives on Justice in America,* edited by Susan Richards Shreve and Porter Shreve, 82–92. Boston: Beacon Press, 1997.

"In the Bamboo Grove: Some Notes on the Poetic Line." In *The Line in Postmodern Poetry,* edited by Robert Frank and Henry Sayre, 83–96. Urbana: University of Illinois Press, 1988.

"In the Charles Wright Museum." *Los Angeles Review of Books,* August 2011. https://lareviewofbooks.org/essay/in-the-charles-wright-museum

"Lost in Place: Longing for the Brave New World of L.A." *LA Weekly,* August 16–22, 1996, 30–32.

"A Man on a Child's Swing: Contemporary Japanese Poetry." In *The Poetry of Our World: An International Anthology of Contemporary Poetry,* edited by Jeffery Paine, 453–57. New York: HarperCollins, 2000.

"Ministry: Looking at Kīlauea." Introduction to *Hot Spots: America's Volcanic Landscapes,* by Diane Cook and Len Jenshel, i–v. Boston: Little, Brown, 1996.

"The Mirror Diary." *Georgia Review* 58, no. 2, special issue on Poetry and "Poiēsis" (Summer 2004): 458–70.
"On Walt Whitman's 'Leaves of Grass.'" *Massachusetts Review* 33, no. 1 (1992): 81–84.
"R.S. Thomas." *Poetry Pilot* (February 1990): 2–5.
"Sea and Scholarship: Confessional Narrative in Charles Olson's 'Maximus, to himself.'" *New England Review and Bread Loaf Quarterly* 8, no. 1 (1985): 118–29.
"'Turning Japanese: Memoirs of a Sansei' by David Mura." *Mānoa: A Pacific Journal of International Writing* 3, no. 2 (1991): 227–29.
Under Western Eyes: Personal Essays from Asian America. Introduction. New York: Anchor/Doubleday, 1995.
"Working for DWP." *Plume*, May 2015: Featured Selection. http://plumepoetry.com/2015/05/featured-selection-13/

Special thanks go to my former graduate students Luke Hollis and Paul Pickering, who helped prepare the manuscript for publication, working long hours for nothing but the gratitude I express here.

For their help with bibliographic research, I want to acknowledge Roy Kamada and Julia Kolchinsky Dasbach.

T.R. Hummer and Kristiana Kahakauwila read and commented on the title essay, which helped me greatly.

For time and the solitude to prepare this manuscript, I owe a debt of gratitude to the MacDowell Colony and the Lucas Artists' Residencies at Villa Montalvo. I am also grateful to the College of Arts and Sciences of the University of Oregon for a Creative Arts Fellowship that funded a term's leave from teaching.

Contents

I

The Mirror Diary

When I was twenty, I decided to dedicate myself to the study of art and literature. It would be as if I were an apprentice in some religious practice, laying down the foundation of learning in letters and values both spiritual and moral that I would draw upon in later days. My yearning was intense, I thought, and my devotion almost absolute. I read and I read and I read, only and all the time. I was away at college, of course, and I was overjoyed. I had escaped the noisy house of my upbringing in Gardena, a postwar Levittown of Los Angeles, a neighborhood crowded with loneliness and working-class anger. I read fiction in the afternoons out on the porches and lawns and poetry in my room after supper in the dining halls. After midnight, with the company of a cup of wine, I practiced calligraphy. In the mornings, I studied languages and read as little as possible in my science texts—the explanations and charts therein befuddled me. I was for literature and that was it. On Botany field trips, I took Shakespeare's comedies and read them on the bus as we swayed along small roadways through the California foothills, spring lupines, purple brushes of salvia, and yellow buttercups burgeoning under the oaks and in the fields around us. Strolling the dusty campgrounds at night, I recited the love lyrics of Sir Thomas Campion and made eyes at the fires of my own learning.

It was, alas, a somewhat hermetic experience. I began to long for things: for companionship, of course, the true thing always elusive—"They flye from me who sometyme did me seeke . . ."; but also, and in the most earnest way, for ancestry, for a sense of descent from noble things, not only from a people, as was being chronicled for me in the novels of William Faulkner, but from a tradition of thought, of speech without desperation or the angry pollutions of human affairs. I who was so filial to the texts of my studies, so observant of the mores and principles both articulated and implied in Boethius and John Gower, was beginning to reflect on the contradiction that I was in no direct way tied to them, to that English cultural tradition. My own people came from southern Japan—in 1888 my grandfather always said, talking about his father's passage. The family came from Hiroshima, Fukuoka, Satsuma, and Wakayama. They were laborers and strike leaders on the sugar plantations in Hawai'i They were a dancer, a tea-house owner, a country storekeeper, and drivers of mules in the cane fields. They were a kind of golden mystery to me at the time. There was no brief of their passage. No record that I knew of that marked their stories down for me to inscribe myself within them as the living image of their ancestral shadows.

And so, before long, I invented a book. In secret. At first, I told no one, but I wrote that it was so in a diary of my own dreaming, as if it were a memory, though I knew I had not lived it, that the book did not exist. But I convinced myself that it did. In my diary, I wrote that I found it when I was five or six, rummaging around in the basement garage of my grandfather's house on Kamehameha Highway on the island of O'ahu near the town of Hau'ula. I had been exploring in the shelves alongside the polished green Chevy, careful to climb up on the floorboards, step on the seat, and push quickly with my bare foot from the dashboard and lowered passenger window on up so I could reach the high shelves crowded with things. My grandfather kept boxes full of sparkplugs, rayon lure skirts, seashells, and beach-washed glass up there out of which he fashioned curios for the tourists. A crèche of toy hula girls in the polished half-shell of a coconut. A kind of Joseph Cornell-box with *opihi*, chips of colored glass, spotted cowries, and a starfish.

There were a few books up there too, mildewing and coated with a fine, powdery black rot: high school yearbooks with teenage pictures of my mother and aunts in them, paperback adventure novels—westerns mostly, and some with fake leather covers in red and green. Their titles were embossed in gold. *For Whom the Bell Tolls. The Great Gatsby. Anna Karenina. The Wisdom of the East.* But, among these, the legacy of my father's postwar subscription to a Reader's Digest Book Club, I told myself I found a storekeeper's ledger—a book made for accounts and balances, for inventories and expenditures, for profits and debts. Yet when I opened it, shaking off its dust, what I discovered instead was a journal—the diary of my learned, neo-Confucian grandfather's—written in *so-shyo*, Japanese calligraphy, a brush-written script like floating lotuses and reeds twisting in a swift stream, beautiful to apprehend but impossible for a child, or any modern, to decipher. I turned page after page, running my fingers down each neat, ribboning column, and I knew that this was sacred, a book of profound secrets.

The pages were yellowed on the edges and blackened near the spine where the stitching was, and they were soft, swollen with moisture from the nearby sea. The writing, composed of stylized ideograms and a linked syllabary, looked to me vaguely like the sutra scrolls the Buddhist priest chanted over at Kahuku temple, only finer, less like rows of black spiders and more like the surface swirls and eddies of Hauʻula Stream as it raced under the WPA Bridge. Another time I took it out, it looked like the banners draped over the sacrifice of *saké* barrels and *shōyu* on festival days, the headbands and flowing sleeves of the evening, fire lit dancers on Bon Odori, the Day of the Dead. The book crackled with esoteric energy.

I stole it. And I kept it with me throughout my days.

From that time in childhood when I snatched it from the garage shelf, through the move from Hawaiʻi to the Mainland, through Boy Scouts and juvenile gangs, football and girls, I kept it. I called it the *kagami nikki*, a title I invented from what I knew from my rudimentary studies of Japanese literature. It meant "The Mirror Diary" and had the ring of medieval essay collections and Tokugawa travel diaries I loved so much. My vow was to become scholarly enough to read it one day. And, when I did, when I had trained myself properly and was ready, it would tell me, like the murmuring ghost of my own grandfather standing behind me in the bedroom's full-length mirror, the unshared secret of who I was and from whom I came.

This was, quite simply, a profound rage for story, for a master tale that justifies, in the powerful way that literatures do, my own presence in my own time in history. Obviously, I had realized that the literature I was studying could not account for that,

that I was not being given "a national tale," a cultural identity that spoke to the convergence of global histories making me a fourth-generation American. Unlike the child in John Steinbeck's Salinas story "The Leader of the People," I could not be ushered into the sweet fiction that my grandfather had come West, leading the wagon trains along the Oregon Trail. And, with little direct knowledge, with almost nothing then available in the archive to study and learn from about we peoples who came from Asia to America, I fabricated my own legend of this grandfather's journal, this invented archive and pioneer's diary, so that I could be, so that I would be worthy of the wisdom of a literature that spoke directly of my own people and not the gross, uncouth, child-of-immigrants Caliban I was afraid I was without it. So, like a lonely child inventing an imaginary friend, I had my book, my ancestral literature after all.

It consoled me for the short while I needed to finish a literature degree in college. I traveled to and lived in a temple in Japan for a year. I did graduate studies in Japanese at a great university, leaving without a degree. I started a theater company in Seattle dedicated to the production of Asian American scripts. I spent a while in Hollywood and hated it. I entered graduate school again, this time to study poetry. I was beginning to write poems of my own and I'd forgotten all about "The Mirror Diary" that had been the comforting fiction of my younger days.

❦

10 July 1919

I went out from Tanaka Store, Kimi, and took a long survey of the workers in the fields, as if for the first time. What drew me was seeing the black plume of smoke from the locomotive and then, when I got closer, the commotion of a mule team dragging the gang plow behind it, kicking up dust and chaff from the old sugar cane lying all over the opened ground. Every day I see these tableaux from the back window of the store whenever I stack boxes or pull them out. Smoke and then dust, whistle and then whipcracks and the braying of animals. But, this time, something within me said I had to go back to the burning fields that I thought I'd left far behind me, witness the labor that I swore at every day that I was made to do it, that my father and mother swore at every day they did theirs. Six days a week, ten hours per day in the hot fields, twelve hours in the sugar mill that was even more hot, sweating over the vats, stacking the cane, grinding them in the machines. Monthly wages— twelve dollah, fifteen dollah. Whistles, bells, sirens. I remember them, Kimi. Work-work, they say, faster-faster. Then Rest, five minutes. Then work-work again, *wiki-wiki.* "Hully up," the *lunas* shout, whipping us with their words. I walk the dirt pathways, step on planking thrown over the sluices and flumes, and hear a worker sing this angry song:

> For our homelands,
> The far islands of the Rising Sun,
> We try to soldier on,
> Carrying the hoe on our sore shoulders
> Instead of rifles,
> Machetes and cane knives in our belts
> Instead of short swords,
> Hate brimming in our hearts
> Instead of love.

He must think of himself as a warrior for Japan, somehow, working so far away in this Owhyee for such few wages. These contract laborers earn only enough to get by, *bango* tags around their necks, making a man a number. They hunker for meals on a patch of cleared caneland. They eat Japan rice and boiled burdock root, sea salt and *limu* for flavor. The singer takes his pride from Japan, from a story of warriors, poor thing. Only the nation when one is so bereft.

Yet, last night, while I was wandering through Camp 7, I heard someone else sing a different tune, with different words, something more mournful—gentle. He must have improvised the words on a teahouse song he heard in town or on the ship on his way over from Yokohama:

I grunt like an animal from Hell
While I hack and slash through the canes
And trample them under my boots.
But, evenings, when I hear the plaintive song of crickets,
I think to leave, just for them,
An island of stalks uncut and whispering
In the soft, tropical winds.

I suppose even a humble worker dressed in denim can express tender feelings like a gentleman poet in *hakama*. Kimi, it is amazing, but I have those feelings too.

While they work, the women sing as well, stripping the drying cane of their leaves, *hore-hore*. In gingham dresses and aprons, they flail with hoes and machetes, straw hats like baskets covering their faces, thick work gloves drenched with sap and oil on their hands. When I look down a row of cane, a *hippari*-man, the pace-setter, hired by the plantation, rushes angrily down it, calling this nagging, scolding song full of insult to the women, who call back from their own rows of cane:

Faster, faster, you whores,
And stop your goddamn grousing.
You can't do honest work
With your mouth!

When they chant back, the proud women throw chaff and sticks over the tops of the cane at the *hippari*-man, trying to slow him down. Not gentle, the insult they sing back to him is sly, but direct:

Why should we keep up
With a sellout like you?
It's you who gets paid
For working your mouth.
Not us.

🌾

It can never be simple for me to try and recall that I wanted, for so long, to be able read from this book, borne out of a youth's desperate wish to hear from the silenced voices of our ancestral history in America. The wishing of it, over the years, was gradually displaced with concern over minor travails, an autobiography of mainstreaming and errands run, a certain professional and middle-class standing accomplished. What "The Mirror Diary" chronicles felt a long ways away sometimes, like it never happened or happened to other people—not my family. But then, some chance, discomfiting encounter would throw me back to that feeling I always had when I was younger, in my teens, hanging around the house in Gardena, doing chores or escaping homework. Rage. I'd snap on the television and Hop Sing would be there in living color, on *Bonanza*, doing his chop-suey English thing, catering to his bosses the ruling Cartwrights, making a damn fool of himself—and me too, I thought. Oriental minstrelsy, *chop-chop*. Or Peter Tong would come on in *Bachelor Father* with his houseboy act, garbling phone messages, *Ikallupusutay*, gooneying for the camera. This was the early sixties, and being Asian was a joke in America—a sidekicking, demeaning one.

I'd want a story about my grandfather then. I'd ask my mother or my aunt when she was visiting—they were always both in a better mood whenever they got together, laughing and carrying on and talking pidgin and remembering the old days in Hawai'i. "What was Papa like back then?" I'd ask, using the name they called him. "What were his routines? How did he know calligraphy? How come he kept so many Japanese books? What did they say? What were they about?"

"We don't remember," they would answer, inevitably. "It was a long time ago. Who cares about that stuff, anyway?"

❦

17 Nov. 1919

Sometimes, Kimi, the comfort women would come through the labor camps all in a wagon together. We would not know much ahead of time if this was to occur, but once word spread, there would be lots of rattling in the tents and shanties—men gathering their coins in tin cans, shaking them at night in anticipation. And the men would gamble, play *hanafuda* all night long, those flower cards, trying to amass the cash to pay for an evening of favor. A man would win and sing this song to the *lunas*, the foremen, and the losers:

> Bossman, there is gambling going on right under your nose,
> And booze brewing out in the far fields,
> And whores doing business by the mountain stream in
>   Camp 9.
> But you're laying stiff and alone in the dark,
> And you can't put a shine on your nose, can you?
> Pumping your hands, kissing the air . . .

Sometimes fights would break out, men would argue and rough each other up, steal the kitty and kick dirt over the weak one who was abused. I heard there would be lines of men sometimes, waiting their turn standing outside a single shanty where the women would be, love sounds inspiring not modesties, but ardor and impatience, the men stamping their feet, rattling coins in their coffee cans, making fun, shouting *wiki-wiki!* at the grunting and *tadaima!* at the climax calls. But the women ever were silent in their suffering and I never knew even one of their names myself. I rented extra blankets from the store those weeks, gave out packets of aspirin powders and ginseng root to the ladies when I saw them.

After the comfort women left, a few of the plantation women would sometimes get a notion to run off, *ha-alele-hana*, and start working that way for themselves:

> Why slave in the cane for pennies
> When I can make a dollar for being on my back,
> Fucking the *paké* man,
> Fucking the Portagee?

I confess I once gave in to acting strangely myself, though not with comfort women. Some years ago, there was a servant woman who would come to the store after she'd lost her job doing her maid work for the wives of the plantation bosses. She would stand a long time in the aisles, looking through the shelves and bins, pulling buckets from underneath, going through the brooms she didn't need and cast iron cookware I knew she couldn't afford. She would dress herself a bit too neatly, as if she were going out to the baths at night—cotton *yukata*, sash, nice slippers. She would never come dirty after work like the field hands. I never saw cane dust or pitch on her once, of course, though I knew—everyone knew—work like that was to be in her future. She'd been accused of stealing or something, and the foreman's wife had let her go. She'd have to start work in the fields again soon, was what people were saying, but maybe not on Kahuku Plantation. She'd have to leave, go to Waialua, or Kāne'ohe. But she was married, her husband a water-man, working the irrigation of the fields, inspecting and repairing sluices and flumes. I'd run into him from time to time, during my saunters. He was tough but small, bandy-legged, and he grew a big moustache. He'd be walking fast along a levee bank, head down, looking at the channel of running water, rubbing mud from his gloved hands, silent and scowling. When I passed him, he'd look up for an instant, ready to accuse, but then see it was me and turn away, without so much as a nod. I was the storekeeper, and though he knew I didn't belong out there in the cane, he couldn't order me. I was beyond his authority, and he depended on my goodwill if he wanted to keep buying food and supplies on credit. I think his name was Kurosawa—"Black Swamp"—a fitting name for a water-man.

One day, while I was stocking the shelves with canned salmon and tuna, I heard a woman's voice, quite softly, singing a little tune unlike the harsh work-songs I was used to by then, not mournful or chantlike either, but like a *saké*-drinking song, light and full of breath and whimsy. I wasn't listening carefully at first, but only picked out stray words here and there. But then I heard her sing the word *wai*, the Hawaiian for "ditch," sung roughly and out of rhythm, but punning, cannily, on the wet channel on the body of a woman. I paid more attention. The sun streamed through the bamboo blinds at the front of the store, cane dust danced in the rays streaming through the slats, and I heard this distinctly, a trickle of sweat springing from my neck and flowing down my chest as she sang:

Tomorrow is Sunday, storekeeper.
Come for my kisses and my hips,
While my husband works the *wai* and waters the cane.
I'll be home by myself soon,
And my lips will be wet for you.

It was hard not to repeat an evil done once, Kimi. I kept it up with her for a while, but I did not steal her. She was gone before the New Year, off to the teahouses in Honolulu a salesman from there said. I do not believe I was the only one to hear her singing.

15 Jan. 1920

It is hot and wearying to walk the fields again, especially after my long absence from the woe of it. When I bent my back, I didn't feel sorrow, only resolve. And thankfulness that I had strength and a plan. I never wanted to stay cutting cane—no one does. Some want a plot of their own to plant from seed and tend to themselves after *pauhana*, work is over. Then, in two years, the company weighs the crop, deducts advance for expenses, and gives you market price. Maybe they still cheat you, but you end up ahead anyway—way ahead than pure labor.

Once I could clearly see the green cliffs of the Koʻolau mountains, jutting walls of rain-worn lavas covered in mosses, I knew it was time to turn back from my survey. From deep within the canefields, I could hear old mule-driver's calls, sung as jokes between work crews, the mule long-gone as a work animal, the crews themselves the mules these days. When I crossed what was left of a burn, stepping over a few stray stalks of stripped and charred cane strewn on the ground, specks of ash afloat in the air like big winter snowflakes in Japan, I heard one last song, this one from a young man, I thought, looking forward to rest and seeing his wife at the end of the day:

Only in this Kingdom of Hell
Are our lives counted by the clock.
But when I come home to you at night,

I cross the River of Heaven
And enter the Domain of Dreams.

❦

I've been told that it's a practice among native peoples to reflect
on ancestral spirits before making any important decision—
particularly things like marriage, accepting a job, quitting one,
adopting a child. And I have a friend in Hawai'i who goes to a
spot on the seashore to chant his ancestral line each time he's
about to make any kind of life change. He says it's to ask their
permission, to ensure his choice is in harmony with them, that
what he does reflects what they have done. If this sounds mere-
ly romantic, perhaps it's because so many of us, as children of
diaspora and citizens of adopted nations, are removed from a
knowledge of our predecessors. Ancestral lives are misty, uncon-
nected to the daily news and our current mortgage rates. Or so
we suppose.

That I wanted this chronicle and had fantasized a legacy of
story had to do with a wish for a similar harmony to my Native
Hawaiian friend's with his own forbears, and it had even more
to do with wishing for a personal dignity in my own time. The
world I grew up in made me feel terribly diminished because of
my race and my lack of history, or, rather, the lack of dissemi-
nated knowledge about that history in the minds of most others
around me. "The Mirror Diary" was my youthful talisman against
the constant cultural white noise of prejudice and ridicule. It
was my private claim of legitimacy in a world that declared me,
like Edmund in *King Lear*, a bastard of history. It was about be-
ing fathered in my own era, sponsored by predecessors I could
pretend were illustrious—epic in a way.

Yet, I suspect that, had I been deprived of this effort of near
lifelong imagining, if I could have, at any time, merely plucked
this volume from my study's bookshelf, read from it casually,
and then returned it to its place amidst other like volumes, I
might have been enacting a colonialist mimicry of Victorian
privilege and manners, an absurd Masterpiece Theater scene
of self-hosting and false welcome of an audience expecting an

ethnic entertainment. That the history is terrible rather than noble, that the book does not exist, my ancestors never wrote and no one much bothered with them enough to transcribe their lives into writing, provides me with the dark watermark of an absence that my current writing must fill. Whatever images I have I inherit from a few photographs of the period—of cane workers arrayed around a locomotive, of my great-grandparents fresh off the boat in Honolulu Bay, of a rainstorm drenching a village of thatched huts amidst an ocean of sugarcane. Whatever words there are of theirs come to me in the real snatches of only a few songs that have survived the cane fields, *hore-hore bushi*, the Hawaiian-Japanese blues borne of unchronicled sufferings, sung by an artist with a creole-Hawaiian name. Like "The Mirror Diary," he is my invention too. I call him Blind-Boy Liliko'i, and, between songs, he swigs a schnapps of passion fruit from a bottle placed beside him on the stage. He plays alternately a *shamisen*, a Dobro, and Hawaiian lap-steel guitar. There is, behind him, a painted backdrop of faded ads for lye-soap and fish markets. He sings the accompaniment to our early history in this country, the music and *meriyasu* for a walking tour through the ghostly rectangles of old labor camps in the midst of stands of abandoned cane, along the spit of a sandy promontory, half-eaten by the sea, studded with wooden grave markers, broken and rotting with a century of age.

"You no write diss," the she-ghosts say, the voices of aged aunts heard in the rasp of the door hinge in the back of my grandfather's old store. "Diss secret, on'y for zah fam-ree."

There was a long stretch when I'd forgotten about "The Mirror Diary." I was building a life, raising a family, trying to make my way. And, as I'd go through my days of teaching classes, running errands, joining my soul to the grocery line and crowds at the movie theaters and fall football games, I found a kind of ephemeral contentment. I married a girl I met in college. I moved from California to Missouri, Missouri to Hawai'i, Hawai'i to Oregon. I collaborated with the other fathers at the tee-ball practices, tossing soft grounders to the boys assembled on the infield in the neighborhood park. I bought an outdoor grill and burned sauce-spackled meats to a sugary crisp. I divorced. My sons grew into tall, jokey adolescents, rowed crew and played football, did passably well in schools. I fell in love with a sassy southerner whose own folk come from the diaspora of the Dust Bowl. I wrote poems of my own and books of my own, but the ghost of the old book that was my necessary history, my invented pride, had slipped quietly away, without thought, as if it were a companion's hand I had just let go of after we'd swum out from shore to reef, and he was drifting now, fairly quickly, caught by the swiftly receding tide and being pulled out to the deepest seas, swept along with all my lost possessions and forgotten errantry.

But, these days, with my sons away at schools, with half a lifetime now behind me, with cousins and college classmates beginning to disappear into the ground and demand their consecrations, this old invented book and legend of an uncompleted self has been returning to me like the rising ghost of a moon that ascends a blank sky in the most brilliant light of day. I've had this need again, to compensate for an absence, to call on my secret prose to describe a seashore, divulge a salty rumor, and tell me a made-up story of scandal and contrition. I want to see the mirror of myself once again as I did when the diary was my nightly pillow.

In the Bamboo Grove

Some Notes on the Poetic Line

The free verse line has been a troublesome and slippery thing to me, defying control and proper description, almost as elusive as what was called "the voice" in the sixties and early seventies. When I studied it, looking at examples from what my teachers (piously or facetiously, depending on their age and fashion of education) called "the canon," it seemed always to make sense, to have integrity, to fit the various styles, and to attach itself to a consistent system of traditional prosody. Even the free verse of T. S. Eliot, the nearly blank verse of the more formal Wallace Stevens, and the improvisations of William Carlos Williams off of a syllabic base all made fair sense and had their own feel and flavor to me, seemed authentic and individual. It was great fun to analyze past practice this way—it was far more difficult to develop a sense of contemporary method and a practice of my own.

With the free verse revival of the sixties, marking its ascendant role in American poetry since, say, the impact of publications like Williams's *Pictures from Brueghel* (1962), James Wright's *The Branch Will Not Break* (1963), and Theodore Roethke's *The Far Field* (1964), free verse has become the normative practice of our day. Because of this development, a host of nontraditional styles have come into print and become popularized, some even equipped with their own bibliographies of theoretical literature explaining their prosodic method, political rebelliousness, and sometimes mystical roots.

As a student, I was both thrilled and puzzled by these innovations—happy because they seemed to want to give literary voice to the American immigrant and working class that, except for Whitman, the free verse patriarch, seemed not to have been granted that voice in the established tradition. But I was as confused as I was happy, even frustrated, while I continued to read essays, attend readings and lectures, engage my friends and, when given the chance, even the proponents themselves in discussions about this new American poetry.

What I didn't understand was that I was wanting to know about style, how a poet constructs a line and shapes syntax around it, and carries the narrative and imagery along too. What was frustrating me was how no one would speak about style as it related to technique, but instead elevated technique over most other concerns. In the extreme background were the ideological wars on the questions of culture and poetic value, many poets unprepared and ineloquent on these matters, the critics for the most part lacking adventurousness, unwilling to give these issues more than a few stray, sarcastic remarks. Much preferred were discussions that made, out of the prosodic eccentricities of a few approved masters, either a science or a mystic undertaking. And it is the legacy of the workshops that, when in doubt about what we are to teach or to uphold, we emphasize and trace the development of *technique*, oftentimes contributing to the trivialization of the genre, raising prosodic and structural fussiness to the level of a fetish-enterprise.

My first poems were written in fairly short, for the most part end-stopped and imagistic lines breaking on the grammatical units of the sentences, themselves fairly short. This gave the poems a choppy yet meditative cadence, I thought, imitating the effect of the Chinese poems in English translation I loved so much. I had been reading Kenneth Rexroth's Tu Fu in the wonderful anthology *Naked Poetry*, my primer in those days, and had recently discovered the magnificent work of Rihaku, Li Po in Chinese, through a pocket-sized edition of Ezra Pound's *Selected Poems* I'd bought at a book sale from a junior who was dropping out to join some commune up in the Santa Cruz mountains. I spent afternoons lying on my back, shirtless on the dormitory's rear lawn, sounding out the rhythms and conjuring the images of this new and beautiful poetic language. I liked how definite the line was as the strongest unit of measure, how it ordered thought as well as phrase, gave the words and sentiments on the right-hand margin as much if not more emphasis as those on the left. The line seemed to cadence the *feeling* as well as the sound. Here's a famous stanza from *Cathay*, largely Pound's Li Po, which appeared in the *Selected Poems* I've already mentioned:

> While my hair was still cut straight across my forehead
> Played I about the front gate, pulling flowers.
> You came by on bamboo stilts, playing horse,
> You walked about my seat, playing with blue plums.
> And we went on living in the village of Chōkan:
> Two small people, without dislike or suspicion.

This is, of course, "The River-Merchant's Wife: A Letter," and it contains, for me, the keys to a method and a style in free verse, coupling the Whitmanic principle of the syntactic and rhythmic integrity of the line with Pound's insistence on an imagistic "hardness" he found in the Provençal and Anglo-Saxon poetry he was also translating at this time. Notice the method of imagistic indirection by way of descriptive statement here, Locke's "simples" as opposed to his "compounds"—what Pound called, in that famous essay he developed from Ernest Fenollosa's notes, the "ideogrammic method." Here also is the Chinese principle of poetic and metaphysical parallelism at work, with the added attraction of the enumerative, complex sentence—a contribution from English rather than the Chinese. These are techniques that have all become the familiar stock-in-trade of free verse practitioners through the Modern and contemporary periods. The style also imports a tender, melancholic tone into English that is at once intimate and nostalgic without being overtly sentimental or formally elegiac as was so much of the late Victorian work against which Pound was trying to rebel. It is a new sound and somehow, for me, it remains as much so as does the saxophone and trumpet of John Coltrane and Miles Davis in the sextet that recorded *Kind of Blue* in the late 1950s.

Over and above the technical and musical lessons I got from Pound and Li Po, I had something else going on with the work—something at the time I thought entirely personal, a bit illegitimate academically, and, therefore, quite thrilling. I enjoyed the private conceit, false as it may have been, that I somehow might be learning an Eastern tradition of composition. As I've said, I hadn't then much affection for the English tradition of metric verse as it was taught me in school—it seemed so much a part of the institutions and ideology that I felt oppressed me, my parents, and grandparents. Neither could I agree with the vision of life and concepts of society and cultural style that seemed ingrained in this Anglo-American tradition. In these ways, there was both a prosodic and a culturally rebellious impulse behind my early efforts at structuring a poetic line.

This strong desire for cultural recuperation combined with a beginner's natural affection for the deceptively simple, prose-like rhythms of the Chinese translations. Here are the lines from the first thing I wrote that I felt confident calling a poem:

Issei:

First-Generation Japanese American

An old man turning pages of books
Left to right. He reads backwards,
Up and down, *kanji* and *kana* script,
Over and over again. He does not see
The old words any more. The meanings
Lost, he pauses on a page and curls
His fingers, surrounding one lone
Character in the cradle of his hand.
He turns, knowing that I watch him
And pity the sleep in his eyes.
This is your name, he says,
We take it from son of prince.
Kaoru is your name.

There are some other things going on here—a sense of the poem as a process of self-discovery and revelation, a somewhat stilted and antiquated diction, the unconscious incorporation of the Chinese tradition of dithyrambic parallelism—but it is significant to me that none of these would have been possible without the measure of this line shaping the progress of the poem. And it is a cultural style somehow tying me to certain learned Asian traditions in the "as if" of the poem, allowing me, imaginatively, to participate in the aesthetics of hanging scrolls, ink paintings, drunken and contemplative poets reveling in nature, scholarship, and each other's company.

My impulses, then, come from an emotional need to feel continuity with a culture in fact discontinuous from that in which I live my everyday life. The line is here as much an imaginative aide as prosodic device, defining a style of writing in a way I couldn't rationally accomplish myself. My sense of the line here verges on the idea of adopting a persona, even assuming a mask as William Butler Yeats may have done, and the result is that somehow a poem gets written, a poem I don't altogether control, and a poem that not only divulges something but which, in the words of the workshop, "makes a discovery" as well. It is a poem which, I hope, is not ruled by what Louis Althusser called the ideological state apparatus, the self-perpetuating institutions and ideologies of the dominant society that tend to reproduce culture *in the form of the same*—the poem having to be like John Donne's or W. H. Auden's or, worse yet, like radio jingles in order to be approved, find publication, and be praised. Yet, it is not a "free" thing in the Kantian sense either, defining its own apartheid realm of consciousness and aesthetic experience. Rather, it is itself an action, albeit a symbolic one, making a counterclaim to authority over individual consciousness, exerting a force in opposition to that manifested by the ads for Gump's or Lucky Strike, or, more consequentially, to those ideas of culture and behavior perpetuated by something like *Magnum P.I.* It is a thing instinct with revolution and the independence of consciousness necessary to extricate itself from the popular mind and to receive its own histories apart from those false, politically accommodating ones prescribed for us by—let me use a metaphor—"the state."

Yet, behind the schemes I was trying to imitate is, nevertheless, a whole storehouse of Western theory and practice. Pound's line in *Cathay* is arguably as much derived from his studies and translations of Provençal and Anglo-Saxon verse as anything in Fenollosa's cribs from Mori and the Chinese. Indeed, his marvelous and sonorously memorable version of "The Seafarer" is included in the original edition of *Cathay*, a strong hint to critics and poets about shared principles of prosody and poetic diction Pound discovered in these otherwise independent traditions. (As I've said, there was an imagistic hardness to both styles, a cleanness of diction, an intensity of emotion expressed with understated, stoical eloquence.) And I suspect that the integrity of the line, its independence as a unit of sound, owed much to Whitman's free verse line. For Rexroth, the relaxed, occasionally enjambed line he used for his versions of Tu Fu were a reflection of his view of the Orient as offering alternative life and poetic styles in opposition to the ostensibly more rigorous, straitlaced, and, to his mind, petrified traditions of the West. Here's a typical piece from the breakthrough book, *One Hundred Poems from the Chinese*, first published in 1956:

Country Cottage

A peasant's shack beside the
Clear River, the rustic gate
Opens on a deserted road.
Weeds grow over the public well.
I loaf in my old clothes. Willow
Branches sway. Flowering trees
Perfume the air. The sun sets
Behind a flock of cormorants,
Drying their black wings along a pier.

Rexroth here disguises the overt parallelism of some of the statements—"A peasant's shack . . ." followed by "the rustic gate," a mention of the poet loafing in old clothes immediately following the image of a well overgrown with weeds—by importing casual, almost arbitrary enjambments. Beginning with the first line, which breaks on "the," interrupting the convention of maintaining syntactic units in free verse, Rexroth's prosodic method here suggests a looseness of form, an idea of a kind of casual flow that puts into poetic practice certain principles borrowed from Taoism perhaps, ideas of *wu-wei*, or "letting be," the noncontention of cosmic forces, the physical laziness of the poet/sage preparing his mind and spirit for enlightenment or maybe, better yet, the moment of pleasure and aesthetic insight offered by the image of the sun setting behind the cormorants drying their black wings along the pier. The staunch religious beliefs (having to do with perception and awareness—*samadhi* and *satori*) and strict imagistic technique is here camouflaged by the seemingly casual yet ultimately cunning breaks in the lines, the flat, enumerative method, and the sly, slow buildup of the image collection to its climax at the poem's end. This method is anticipated by Pound's "ply-over-ply," his idea of poetry as tapestry and montage that he may have best exemplified in the stunning performance of "Canto IV." Yet, for all its exotic dress in virtuosic imagery, the sentiment expressed in Rexroth's Tu Fu is as much within a Western as an Eastern tradition, the view with regard to rationalism and ideas of imposed order emerging out of the tradition of Western romantic Orientalism prevalent in the literature from Samuel Taylor Coleridge to Allen Ginsberg, Ralph Waldo Emerson to Gary Snyder, and has perhaps as much to do with a healthy antinomianism as with any established Eastern traditions. Nevertheless, these styles and attitudes appealed to me and were a strong inspiration. The line here seemed a key to a separate, alternate system of ethical, spiritual, and aesthetic values I felt more in sympathy with than those prescribed for me elsewhere in my education. It seemed then the central code to a civilization that upheld noble sentiment and endorsed literary values as a primary necessity. I simply wanted to be part of that civilization, and using this poetic line was a way I thought I could be.

Here are other lines, also from a fairly early poem of mine, written perhaps in more conscious imitation of the "Chinese style" I'd come to identify:

The night surrounds me in a dark grey fog.
I feel its chill even under my *futon*.
The *tatami* underneath stiffens my spine.
I am tense and rise to snap on the light,
Set her photographs out before me on the floor.
I take out the old cardboard *hana* cards
My grandfather gave me and pretend she is here
To play this game of old men and young lovers.

The cards show me prints of the wooden sailboat
Piled up to its masts with cherry blossoms.
Young Prince Genji dips his umbrella
To acknowledge the small orange frog
Playing among the pine boughs by the river.
The crane of a thousand days

Considers the swollen red sun of dusk.
Brown ducks fly in a triad over a charred field . . .
    (from "A Restless Night")

These lines are a bit longer, more dense with images, more scru-
pulously parallel and enumerative—poetic catalogue is here a
basis of compositional order. The models are from translations of
Chinese nature and recluse poetry, from Wang Wei, T'ao Ch'ien,
Han Shan, and others I'd read in Cyril Birch's *Anthology of Chinese
Literature* and in studies by James Robert Hightower and J. D.
Frodsham in the Oxford series. In the Chinese catalogue, the
items add up to serve as a sign of the poet's inner melancholy, his
sadness at departure from home and separation from his family
or a lover. The landscape supplies signifiers for his woe, and the
line gives them their syntactic and musical order.

Compare my lines above to these of Witter Bynner's, that fine
Modernist and translator, like Pound, of the T'ang Chinese.
Here's his version, after an eremitic piece by the Buddhist poet
Wang Wei. It's from another great primer of mine, a book origi-
nally published as *The Jade Mountain*, the anthology of 300 in-
dispensable poems of the late T'ang, recently reprinted as *The
Chinese Translations*:

In My Lodge at Wang-Ch'uan after a Long Rain

The woods have stored the rain, and slow comes the smoke
As rice is cooked on faggots and carried to the fields;
Over the quiet marsh-land flies a white egret,
And mango-birds are singing in full summer trees. . . .

I have learned to watch in peace the mountain morning-
    glory,
To eat split dewy sunflower-seeds under a bough of pine,
To yield the post of honour to any boor at all . . .
Why should I frighten sea-gulls, even with a thought?
    (from *The Jade Mountain*)

In Bynner's Wang Wei, the catalogue of landscape details con-
tributes its own imagistic beauty to the poem as well as estab-
lishes the pleasing prosodic effect of a list, parallel events and

images delivered in a sequence of lines roughly equivalent in rhythm and length, made dramatically and syntactically equivalent as well. There's a verbal *and* emotional symmetry at work here, a kind of visual and rhythmic cadence to go along with the poem's theme of equanimity and its endorsement of a humble, quietistic life. The first four lines give us the apprehension, the second four the analysis and resolve—I don't say resolution. The landscape provides exempla for a consolational proof.

There was also a tradition of Chinese poetry composed by Japanese, a kind of Latin for the culture, flourishing at various times from the seventh through the eighteenth centuries, practiced largely by state scholars early on, and then later by Buddhist monks and lay atavists. It is known generically as *kan-shi*, or simply translated, "Chinese poetry." During a certain period from the late Kamakura to the early Muromachi shogunates (roughly, the thirteenth to the fifteenth centuries), it was also known as *Gozan bungaku*, or "Literature of the Five Mountains," in reference to the major Zen temples of the time, traditionally called mountains or mountain dwellings. Whatever the poetry was called, the aim was not so much to be innovative as it was to sound as authentically "Chinese" as possible. Nevertheless, there were a few originals—Sugawara, Kamo no Chōmei, Ryōkan, and Gensei—who managed to get something of themselves, their times, and their land into the work. It's to these masters I owe another debt.

My later poems were to take on other subjects—family, Asian American history, my travels in Japan—and my line changed to suit these different tonal and emotional requirements. The family poems are higher pitched, enjambed, the lines somehow more individually and freely variable, tending to three or four beats. What guided me then was an idea of intensity and propriety I learned from blues and gospel music, the controlled hollers and performance anguish of the soul singer. I remember listening to Johnny Winter's "Drown in My Own Tears" over and over again as I wrote these lines for my father:

I wanted to take away the pain
in his legs, the swelling in his joints,
give him back his hearing,

clear and crystal chimes,
the fins of glass that wrinkled
and sparked the air with their sound.

I wanted to heal the sores that work
and war had sent to him,
let him play catch in the backyard
with me, tossing a tennis ball
past papaya trees without the shoulders
of pain shrugging back his arms.

I wanted to become a doctor of pure magic,
to string a necklace of sweet words
fragrant as pine needles and plumeria,
fragrant as the bread my mother baked,
place it like a lei of cowrie shells
and *pikake* flowers around my father's neck,
and chant him a blessing, a sutra.
    (from "What For")

It may be that formal systems have less to do with lineation than something that's simply intuited, like improvisations off the melody and measure sung by the tenor lead in a street choir.

The line, for me, has to be tied to an idea of a "feeling"—*blues with a feeling*, my brother sang, playing his Les Paul back in that vacant storefront on Gardena Boulevard. It sets an emotional and musical tone to things throughout the poem, mysteriously, and at the same time, works a magical *change* upon common usage to the point that the words, the whole progress of the short utterance that is the poem, gain a marvelous new value, significance, and force. Language thus becomes ceremonial.

The blues, in its emotionally basic and rough-cut yet prosodically sophisticated way, has always been powerful for me, capable, in a short sequence of refrain and variation, to make the recollection of pain and disappointment somehow glorious. I see this power in lines throughout the tradition from Leadbelly to Howlin' Wolf, from Revered Gary Davis to Blind Willie McTell. These cunningly simple lyrics have the magical capacity of giving form and a measure of moral authority to an experience that, without the transformational power of the blues, would otherwise be quite devastating. Here is a lyric by Robert Johnson, a genius of the blues and its ritual powers:

I went down to the crossroads,
Fell down on my knees.

Down to the crossroads,
Fell down on my knees.

Ask the Lord above for mercy,
Say boy, if you please.

Here is the basic verse-unit of the blues: a two-line stanza, a repeat, and then a third stanza with end line rhyming with the second line of the first stanza. This is language raised by artifice to be just that little touch strange and full of symbolic potency. The first two lines set up a rhythm that is then transformed into expectation, that slight bit of suspense, by its being repeated in the following stanza—the classic refrain technique of basic blues. Then, the third stanza closes off the verse-unit with a rhyme and brings the tiny narrative to a close as well, resolving the story with a witty or, in this case, a portentous and sacramental turn of phrase and event. The lines themselves possess the rhythmic and syntactic integrity we admire in Whitman, yet they're composed on a shorter, perhaps more flexible measure. The "feeling" might be carried in the vernacular, subculture diction as well as the quasi-religious symbolism. But I believe it is as much the intensity of the experience it refers to, added to the fact that the blues employs the language of the people who live that experience, that gives these lines their "feeling," their moral and spiritual authority, *and* their prosodic attraction. Subtle syncopations are at work here, the verbal ingenuity of the final line, the penultimate line overloading the measure with a higher syllabic count, necessitating a shift in the pattern of conventional accentuating in speech to the point that the words receive an abnormal, though entirely attractive, pattern of accent and enunciation, displaying a singer/composer's skill, verbal ingenuity, fine ear, and sense of an ending. Aficionados will recall Eric Clapton's version of Johnson's classic song, cherish how this Briton worked a slow-hand change of his own into the lyric:

I went down to the crossroads,
Fell down on my knees.

Down to the crossroads,
Fell down on my knees.

Asked someone above for mercy,
Take me if you please.
(from Cream, *Wheels of Fire*)

In either version, Johnson original or Cream cover, the line displays the rhythmic genius of the blues tradition for reshaping a folk or street sense of language into a ceremonial that has, through the power of pop culture, now entered into the twentieth-century art tradition, giving us a sense of language and sentiment we would not otherwise have—a sense of syncopation, testifying, and talking trash.

The sound pattern in Johnson's blues shapes the lyric, the call for *music* compelling the character and delivery of the words. Yeats talked about a similar kind of thing—I think it was in the *The Autobiography of William Butler Yeats*—when he confessed a poem came first as a vague but compelling "chune" he intuited but could not sing. I believe it can also be linked to cadence, a stress pattern, maybe even Pound's "absolute rhythm" fitted to Robert Frost's psychic "tightening in the throat." It helps set the mode of the composition, the major style of the writing the way a scale and tempo might for a piece of music. Indeed, the line seems tied to what jazz musicians mean when they talk about rhythms, scales, intervals, and the like possessed or embodied of a *feeling*, "like a waltz against 4/4—that quarter/triplet feeling," as Charles Mingus once said.

Even with free verse, the line functions as the last holdover from traditional prosody at the same time that it serves as the primary unit of the new—Pound's composition "in the sequence of the musical phrase, not in the sequence of a metronome." Psychologically, that right-hand margin, arbitrary as it might seem, nevertheless functions to make necessary an adjustment of the *sound* and pace of the writing, a perceptible (and even, in an earlier time, *measurable*) coordination of syntax and stress-pattern to the length of the line, so that common speech is averted, heightened, *strangified*, and the poem becomes a distinctly separate thing.

My later studies introduced other techniques—syllabics, blank and accentual verse, some post-Modernist innovative schemes—but the constant has always been, has had to be, my sense of the *felt* measure as defined by the line, a sense of limit that orders syntax, parcels the narrative, and calls forth from me a largely imagistic diction freely derived from those Modern translations of Chinese poetry.

My current practice combines a variety of lineation methods, breaking on the phrase or clause at times, sometimes enjambed, varying from two to six beats as I like. I could be accused of sloppiness, or worse yet, capriciousness, but I think what I'm doing is working in even more variation and improvisation upon an agreed base in sound and measure I've already established with myself—I know how I sound and I'm trying to work *off* of it, play against my established beat some, and keep things interesting for myself as I write. Here are some lines from the beginning of a recent poem:

> At the No. 1 Café, waiting for his lunch
> of boiled noodles and sliced fishcake,
> the thirtyish man smoking his Chesterfields
> down to the filters is sorting through his worries,
> thinking about the deductible on his dental coverage,
> and deciding, for the moment, that he might
> sacrifice an aching molar to the impassive
> gods of industry and conspicuous consumption.
> *Floor mats*, he sighs, blowing smoke like a bad valve,
> *Brand-name shoes*, his chant against the Fifties
> and the marketing techniques of Sears, Roebuck . . .
>   (from "The Sound of Water")

And some closing lines from my newest poem, done last week in Hawai'i:

> . . . I cough too much, can't smoke or drink
> or tend to things. Mornings, I roll
> myself off the damp bed, wrap

a blanket on, slip into wooden clogs,
and take a walk around my pond and gardens.
On this half-acre, calla lilies in bloom,
cream-white cups swollen with milk,
heavy on their stems and rocking in the slight wind,
cranes coming to rest on the wet, coppery soil.
The lotuses ride, tiny flamingoes, sapphired
Pavilions buoyed on their green keels on the pond.
My fish follow me, snorting to be fed,
gold flashes and streaks of color
like blood satin and brocade in the algaed waters.
And when the sky empties of its many lights,
I see the quarter moon, horned junk
sailing over Ka'ū and the crater rim.
This is the River of Heaven . . .
    (from "The Unreal Dwelling: My Years in Volcano")

I wouldn't do this, of course, without the security of feeling and knowing how I like things to sound, without some idea of what workshops call "the voice."

The line was, I believe, my beginning to finding a measure and a sense of voice, but now it's as much an intuited thing that provides a pace for my written speech. It's almost like a character now, a persona or mask as Yeats explained it, that sets the time and calls forth the writing. And that character seems to mediate between me and those cultures I burn to belong to. A kind of sage or patriarchal muse, he has less formal knowledge than I, absolutely no scholarly training, but wisdom in areas I don't—folklore, traditional Asian arts, ancient religions. And he governs himself more by instinct than by learning or necessity, possessing both an absolute freedom and esoteric discipline.

And so practice remains a mystery to me and a delight. I try to know less as I learn more—teaching my students more in terms of technique, tradition, and critical thinking than I would allow myself to hold in my head as I write. Still, those things are there, intuited and hopefully strong at the level of the subconscious. Ultimately, the line has to be not simply a unit of measure, but a unit of *feeling*, a way to begin the invocation of larger systems—call it race memory, a historic or psycholinguistic unconscious—that constitute the true and actual eminent powers behind poetry.

Sea and Scholarship

Confessional Narrative in Charles Olson's
"Maximus, to himself"

I return to this poem from a long distance and span of time, having first read it in college one spring in California when the oaks on campus were blooming with chandeliers of pollen, their mustard-brown sprays of stamen-and-pistil a potent testament to the renewal and resurrection in the natural world. My girlfriend was gleeful, happily absorbed in Gustav Mahler, rehearsing for a spring symphony concert, and I was full of joy myself, reading in Mahayana scripture and D. T. Suzuki's commentary, everything somehow suddenly solvable and potentially righteous though the war dwindled on and Watergate was taking over the news. Olson's poem seemed then a summation to a large, worldly experience, a testimony of an entire life lived, finally, coherently, after a long struggle with warring impulses and youthful blundering. Maximus, as a character, appeared to possess and impart a hard-won earthly wisdom, yet to point toward a further project beyond his previous experience, a project partaking of the heroic, the spiritual, some great "other" beyond normal ken. It was a poem grander than its complex and diverse experience, a life both of manual labor *and* of scholarship. As I've been trying to say, it was for me a very *together* piece of writing.

The poem stayed with me through senior exams and a summer working for L.A.'s Water and Power, reading electric meters in San Pedro and walking almost every square foot of city land there. It stayed with me through a year in Japan, my first real winter, and a spring trying to follow Bashō's narrow road through the north country backroads of Honshu. *The Maximus Poems*—that Jargon/Corinth paperback with the seachart cover and blue titling—was always somewhere in my tote, a literary map and compass, even abroad.

What I first liked about it was how brave it was in revealing its speaker's character, his own assessment of the flaws and accomplishments of his life, the evenhandedness of his judgments. The poem seemed a patient and serious gathering together of the self, an orderly act of assemblage and of judgment. It was a *confession*, a condensed narrative about the evolution of an identity, a contemporary heir to the literary tradition established by Augustine, continued through William Wordsworth, Jean-Jacques Rousseau, and Maksim Gorky, up to Victorian and Modern lyric cousins of the form I see in Alfred Tennyson and Pound.[1] I didn't know this then, but the poem has stuck in my mind through the circuitous wanderings of my own literary education, and resurfaces here, twelve years after Commencement, as an example of a lyric mode that I'm going to identify as the *confessional narrative*.

In confession, the writer returns through the power of memory to lost moments of his past, meditates upon them, and confronts both the good and bad (or the beautiful and ugly) elements of his own character, and works out a complex, momentary psychic resolution to the dissonant and fragmentary impulses churned up by his acts of recollecting and telling. Something cathartic occurs, the expulsion of some psychic poison that has absorbed whatever had been previously retarding the growth of the soul towards its rightful splendor, and the writer's consciousness then gains its momentary amplitude. It was thus with Augustine, his writing cutting through his guilt and confusion about past deeds, establishing a continuity and progress of spiritual education when looked at in retrospect, adding up to a journey toward his acceptance of faith and his reconciliation, not so much with his past self (although this becomes the emphasis of secular confession), but with his God.[2] In Augustine's *Confessions*, there is an almost Aristotelian progress (the narrative obeying the laws of necessity as Augustine moves toward accepting Christianity, strengthening his faith) whereby Augustine, as narrator and character, sorts through the swarm of his past experience and picks out the elements of cohesion and continuity, bringing about the recognition of faith and his own moral consciousness.[3] Yet it is not the "coming-of-age" story, a *bildungsroman* or progress toward maturity. It is rather an intense and orderly recollection, a spiritual memoir, the informed, mature narrator looking back in retrospect over his own life and constructing a coherent autobiography with the dire earnestness of philosophic inquiry and spiritual practice.

Likewise in Wordsworth's autobiographical poem, *The Prelude*, the poet looks back to geographically scattered and temporally disparate moments in his life and infuses them all with his retrospective vision of coherence, joining them together not only by the thread of his own biography, but by constructing around them a narrative of spiritual continuity and repetition—his theme about the natural world as wedded to man's mind and his ideal that, periodically, through "spots of time," this crucial awareness through the visitation of a grander consciousness would make its impression upon private consciousness. Wordsworth's poem reconstructs the past, and his imagination is assigned redemptive force, retrieving and illuminating various events in the chronicle from boyhood to maturity, bringing them together in a focused consort of shared spiritual origin and imaginative purpose. His vision subsumes all temporal (and potential psychological) difference under the overall narrative—the growth of the poet's mind. Thus all events are brought into clear relation and given their ultimate meaning as validations of the growth and authority of the poetic imagination, inhabiting and constructing the poem at the same time as it constructs and reveals itself in the act of writing.

In both Wordsworth and Augustine I see *narratives* in which a self previously mysterious, certainly uncertain, is *arrived at, constructed* in the retrospective meditation upon past acts. An identity is built or revealed, a continuity discerned, and a pattern perceived. The narrative orders the past into a story of progress, with the consciousness revealed or arrived at in the present of the poem itself acting as a kind of glorious end point, a narrative and psychological *telos* to all previous events. My notion here of poetic composition differs from Frost's idea of "a momentary stay against confusion"; by up until now discussing only such lengthy, almost epic confessional texts, I have seen that moment as extended and dispersed throughout the entire poem so that the stay is no longer momentary, but monumental. I am, in fact, making a distinction between the aesthetic (and perhaps psychological) force of a piece of literary narrative as opposed to the power of the short lyric—that is, in narrative the "stay" is longer, organizes more information and psychic dissonance.

In Olson's poem, though it is a shorter, lyrically condensed piece and not the lengthy confessional epic constructed by Wordsworth or Augustine, the narrative functions in a similar way. Maximus speaks from a mature perspective, reflecting back on past acts of failure and accomplishment in a voice so modest it is eloquent. Let's look at the whole piece:

I have had to learn the simplest things
last. Which made for difficulties.
Even at sea I was slow, to get the hand out, or to cross
a wet deck.
      The sea was not, finally, my trade.
But even my trade, at it, I stood estranged
from that which was most familiar. Was delayed,
and not content with the man's argument
that such postponement
is now the nature of
obedience,
        that we are all late
        in a slow time
        that we grow up many
        And the single
        is not easily
        known

It could be, though the sharpness (the *achiote*)
I note in others,
makes more sense
than my own distances. The agilities

        they show daily
        who do the world's
        businesses
        And who do nature's
        as I have no sense
        I have done either

I have made dialogues,
have discussed ancient texts,
have thrown what light I could, offered
what pleasures
doceat allows

But the known?
This, I have had to be given,
a life, love, and from one man
the world.
Tokens.
But sitting here
I look out as a wind
and water man, testing
And missing
some proof

I know the quarters
of the weather, where it comes from,
where it goes. But the stem of me,
this I took from their welcome,
or their rejection, of me

And my arrogance
Was neither diminished
nor increased,
by the communication

2

It is undone business
I speak of, this morning,
with the sea
stretching out
from my feet[4]

Maximus looks back in summary and assessment of his life, he
makes judgments, evaluates his actions and direction, ties to-
gether disparate experiences—some time at sea, a life spent,
finally, involved with scholarship of some kind ("I have made
dialogues, / discussed ancient texts, . . .")—in the act of self-

contemplation that is the poem. The narrative here involves the discernment of continuity and purpose in the life, the arrival at the pleasant, equanimous consciousness that utters this speech about itself. In other words, a *self* is constructed in the course of speaking reflectively about the self, fragmentary elements from the past, perhaps distanced for one reason or another (". . . I stood estranged / from that which was most familiar"), are taken up in the course of the poem, considered and reconciled in felt, intuitive connections to the sanguine imagination of the poem. It is Maximus, to himself, speaking with a subdued and cheerful brevity about his lifelong project of self-seeking and self-creation.

I have already defined the "spine" of Olson's poem, its discernible if somewhat vague narrative plotting, as the construction and evolution of a mature poetic consciousness.[5] This is the good scaffolding upon which other riches are built, grand associations made. Each moment of self-definition in the poem is followed by a compelling dismissal of an apparently widely held commonplace about the nature of worldly experience. Maximus draws from himself, his assessment of his progress and struggle through the world, some interesting pronouncements that sum up his costly lessons.

Maximus had begun with several admissions—that he's "had to learn the simplest things last," that, at sea, he was "slow to get the hand out" and that, in fact, the "sea was not, finally [his] trade." It's a splendid introductory strategy. We like him, this character Maximus speaking to us, like him right away for being able to confess his shortcomings without self-pity or defensiveness. He speaks simply of his nature, what he's learned he can't do, and his forthright admission charms us. But this is a beginning that prepares us well for the rest, gaining our sympathy and attention—he's obviously a man who's been around the dock, a man of humility, possessed of the kind of self-awareness that experience brings—so that the statements of the second stanza come off as considered opinions and protestations, the objections of a reasonable man. ". . . I stood estranged / from that which was most familiar," says Maximus, "was delayed, . . ." And then launches into a string of discontentments, his admission to a deep quarrel with what seems to be a worldview that might otherwise dominate him, repress his true nature, retard the development of his good character.

> and not content with the man's argument
> that such postponement
> is now the nature of
> obedience,
>> that we are all late
>> in a slow time,
>> that we grow up many
>> And the single
>> is not easily
>> known

He repudiates "the man's argument," confesses to a misanthropic perspective on the common wisdoms of his age, admits to possessing what might be called, romantically, the poet's dissenting character. (Elsewhere, Randall Jarrell made of this perspective a major statement against American culture, what he confessed to be his "sad heart at the supermarket.") Maximus does not agree that his "slowness" was beneficial in the sense that it was one of the consequences of learning *obedience*, a submission to social or perhaps spiritual authority. He does not agree that his time is a bad one within which all are somehow lacking, an age of cultural and moral decline perhaps. And he cannot accept the argument that we are loose fragments, politically anarchistic, and that forming a single body, a political and spiritual commonwealth, a *polis*, is impossible. His is a magnificent minority perspective, not content with received notions, nor with keeping company with the throng "who do the world's / business. . . ."

There are also strong neo-Platonic echoes here, "the single" he cites cryptically ringing heavily of "the one" in Plotinus, the *hēn* of the realm of the eternals that organizes and suffuses all things and was a principle of Manicheanism. Maximus's sympathies are with these kinds of political and philosophic idealisms, his ambitions for a doubled inner and outer order, the enlightened political organization of society as well as his own psychic unity.

But what's he done, ultimately, with his life?—worked with

texts, been a scholar and philosopher; so we gather from how he admits to having "discussed ancient texts," fashioned dialogues of his own. And we can tell from the manner of his saying that the dialogues would have been Socratic and not Sophoclean, that is, philosophic and not so much dramatic entertainments. Working with the unknown, he's done fairly well, but admits that he's had trouble with "the known"—referring perhaps to the commonplace learning most of us acquire earlier or more easily. Maximus calls these "tokens," suggesting that his cherished quotidiana, his exoteric knowledge, might be emblems of some *other* where his real interests, real truth, some grandly luminous flower of *being* all lie spinning slowly in his subconscious and the *to-be-revealed* of this poem. Read this way, "the known" that he has had to be given, is declared to be representative of the higher order, metonyms of the *hēn*, the one, the singularity Maximus seemed to be yearning for early on in this poem and, indeed, early on in his setting out to sea and scholarship. This seems to be a kind of homespun but noble Yankee Heideggerianism, a wish for revelation in the working through of things—texts, an act at sea, the specific utterance of this short speech—intellectual and aesthetic sublation, a rising above manifold reality to partake of its hidden order. There is an idea of ritual here, its efficacy and necessity, and also a kind of faith that whatever it is that is the *one* can be gotten to through decent scholarship and decent living. It's a kind of scholastic mysticism, though without the monkish rejection of all the world's contingencies and frayed blessings. Maximus is "a wind and water man" after all, and he holds book and sea as equal realms of his education. To me, as a college senior trying to put together a culture for myself, these ideas didn't seem very far from certain Buddhist notions of *karma, samsara, samadhi, nirvana* and all their interworkings.[6] The combination here, in Maximus, of spiritual yearning and a journeyman's experience, of training in both, also seemed to me analogous to the principles of education I admired in the meditative Buddhism I was trying to practice. In this way, "Maximus, to himself" was, for me, a kind of modest *summa* for my own values and expectations, and I responded to the poem as I might have to the casually spoken wisdoms of a master tradesman or religious teacher.

The poem then shifts gears, Maximus saying "But sitting here / I look out as a wind / and water man . . . ," the switch of reference and of tone like a slight shift in the wind coming from a new compass-point, quickening our readerly senses and marking the beginning of Olson's end-music to the poem. We sense recurrence here, the recapitulation of elements we've been introduced to before. Maximus claims to know "the quarters / of the weather," and this deft turning from his remarks on scholarship to the new claims of acquaintanceship with the natural world marks a charming return to the subject of his opening statements about his relations with the sea. He acknowledges the life of labor, roughneck experience on or near the sea. He *derives* from it, he says, "the stem of me . . . [which I] took from their welcome / or their rejection, of me . . . ." He's kept his natural impulses, his arrogance and indivisibility. The feeling of accumulated experience and its consequent sagacity is very much heightened here. I felt then, as I do almost every time I read this poem, that something very important is about to be told, that I may bring a small measure of reverence to my reading of these last strophes.

And reverence seems to me to be what this poem has been about—a respectful attitude toward one's own life and toward the world one lives in, a calm but constant sense of awe at natural phenomena and the accumulated wisdom of literary culture. But more than any of these things, I think now that the topic has been, or, perhaps more accurately, the *discovery* has been, an idea of reverence in and for measured *speech*, for a discourse elevated in a slight but casually ceremonious way above that of common practice, a manner of talk taken out of its quality of dailiness and removed, through an artfulness acquired from learning and worldly experience, to a level that partakes of ritual, a separate order. This is an idea of sacerdotal speech, of spiritually empowered discourse, of almost supernatural utterance that, in the poem, comes through in its contemplative and melancholic tones (a trick and attitude John Milton celebrated in "Il Penseroso"), in the chain of cryptic wisdoms denied early on, following the pessimism and rhetorical method of Ecclesiastes's antisermonizing preacher.

I am not talking about anything like the revealed word or of a paganistic idea of *vates* and the power of oracles—these seem to me to be more extreme cases of sacred speech and make a more ambitious and direct claim to value as truth than I think poetry generally makes—yet I do believe what I'm saying relates to these uses of language. Olson's way of using well-considered words, his elevated tone, the confessional subject, and a retrospective point of view shares with these other forms of discourse the very clear idea of momentousness and ceremony in language. The poem itself is one utterance, a short speech summarizing the polarities of an interesting though not uncommon life, taking care to give its integrity the proper characterization, and recognizing throughout the importance and seriousness of this act. It is one spoken event and has continuity as such, reflecting the compositional laws of Aristotelian propriety, staying close to normal idiom while not reluctant to import the occasional rare word, the ornamental phrase. In the main because it is so considered and skillful in its utterances, I think the overall poem gives off an unmistakable kingliness of tone and shares with Tennyson's "Ulysses" not only a seafaring subject but also a measure of grandiloquence. Like Tennyson's Ulysses, Olson's Maximus speaks with great tonal dignity, a sense of momentous occasion, not simply of the upcoming event, but also of the event of his self-consideration, his address to himself and to us, his unnamed hearers, a kind of posterity. Both Ulysses and Maximus have their attention fixed upon some great hidden and sublime thing; both hint at the monstrous sea—perhaps a metonym for the future—as both boon companion and splendid adversary. When they speak of an adventure that is itself an ennobling act, their words echo this speech-charmed inspiration, reflecting the heroic dimensions of their visions.

As with Tennyson's poem, "Maximus, to himself" closes with a statement about expectation, prospects viewed with optimism though spoken of merely as "undone business." I see in this last strophe Olson's contemplation of his epic project—the writing of *The Maximus Poems*—joined to the discovery of his own felt geographic and textual *archē*, a multiple origin in poetic speech, gimcrack cabalistic scholarship, and the topographic history of Gloucester, Massachusetts. It is a noble project, the epic of a poet's own self-creation and his textual wedding to a chosen city, his *polis*. And this itself seems ample reason for Maximus's expectant attitude toward the future, most of the project still ahead, stretching out before him like the open sea, a good analogue to the open road of Whitman's nineteenth-century American democracy. The poem thus functions as a short and ceremonial, propitious send-off for the long haul ahead, Olson's own Yankee barcarole, self-commissioned and self-received, on the momentousness of the embarkation.

This essay has stressed coherences—of narrative, of evolved authorial identity, of theme and of tone. I've tried to show how the confessional method constructs its own kind of narrative, associating the temporally and temperamentally disparate events in a life in such a way as to constitute a plotting toward the climax of achieved identity in the literary text, suggesting a kind of retrospective exemplification of the concepts of narrative probability and necessity discussed in Aristotle's *Poetics*.[7] For confession and memoir are in an inverse relation to tragedy, which has as *its* action a moving forward from event (and consciousness) to future events, operating without the direction of a retrospective glance. Unlike tragic drama, the confession builds its coherence out of a life's events, its plot of character building, as the long narrative foreground to the arrival at a present consciousness that, unlike Orpheus's, can redeem its future *only* after looking backward. And though the effects of the confessional narrative are very often cathartic, we do not have to suffer the destruction of the hero in order to achieve it, this *pharmacosis* occurring in fact upon the character, the speaker of the poem, and not directly in the audience except through the complicated process of the psychic identification that the act of reading performs. The action achieved here is one opposite from that dismemberment accomplished in Dionysian revels.

Confession is, as I've tried to suggest, a comedy of reconciliation—of the self to its past, of consciousness to all its diverse influences in phenomena, memory, and perception. And the poem itself provides this conciliatory act, becoming in Olson's works the single out of the many, the thing well made out of the complexities and discontinuities that plague life and mind, dispersing the *one* (the *hēn* of Plotinus) into the distanced and tawdry fragments of anomie. What Coleridge lamented in his

"Dejection: An Ode," Olson is able to overcome in "Maximus, to himself." For the moment of the poem anyway, Maximus belongs to himself and to his world in a way all of us, including Wordsworth, might envy.

In my own life I was trying to accomplish something like this belonging I found in Olson's poem. I had wanted from even earlier on than my college days (though that was when these hankerings became most acute—a function, I suppose now, of "senioritis") to bring together the widely divergent cultures and experiences in my own life that I felt at nasty odds with each other, perhaps to construct, in a style of dress or of speech, in a poem or even something as silly to me then as a career, an emblem that would be at once the key to and the accomplishment of—Augustine's pretension and retention—a foregrounded narrative of my own self-creation.[8]

By the next fall, after Commencement, I was still muddling through these desires, traipsing the gravel pathways through the moss gardens and cloud-leaf maples of Shōkoku-ji, still without a poem as good as Olson's. I recall one nightfall in particular, after a day spent gassing with a poet-elder in a Kyoto coffee-house, when the world around me seemed suddenly a living body, street-sellers' calls and the toll of temple bells all the most glorious speech and chant of the galaxy. I realized that scholarship might be a kind of housekeeping in preparation for a visitation; that labor, the work at sea or in cities as was my experience, was a primal necessity crucial for kinetic sympathy with the physical world, and that both activities were subordinate to true sentient experience, the awareness and the exercise of the noumenal powers in the natural world, the body, and the imagination. My naive meditations on the meanings of those mysterious Japanese aesthetic terms suddenly, though briefly, made a little more sense. *Sabi, yōembi, mono-no-aware*, and *yūgen* had a bit more emotional force insofar as they had become, for the moment of my walk and in the aftermath of some frustrating hours of study, *material presences* in my life.[9] There was elegance for me in the flight of an owl as it drifted back to its perch in the cedar tree by the main hall. Sadness seemed to flow from the red ember of the cigarette a cyclist smoked as he rode past. And the stars drenched everything in their silky light, giving every item in sight a new and deeper mystery as the constellations creaked into motion, wheeling above me.

Olson's Maximus, because he has had and draws from both the sea and scholarly experience, has possession of the kind of magnanimity and inner harmony prized by Confucius as the "great learning," a combination of practical knowledge, moral sense, and cultural refinement. It is *jen*, a human goodness he supposed instinctual in us all, to be nurtured through proper education, a truth revealed in all the best poetry. Yvor Winters too, crotchety as he was, mistaken as I think he was in using it as both a measuring stick and a strop, upheld this same notion as an ideal of poetic value when the insisted that a poem be about person's experience *plus* what he or she thinks about it, exercising moral judgment on the event.[10] This is what I like about poetry too—that it makes decisions, moral and spiritual, that it pulls things together, performs that "momentary stay" Frost talked about, and that it gives me both a sense of grandeur and of calm in challenging and quickening both the scholar and the laborer in me.

I'm more than a decade older than when I first read Olson's poem, cultural worlds and half a continent away from the California that was my backdrop for its initial reading. The Midwest surrounds me now—the chirping drone from throngs of thirteen-year cicadas swirls from the sweet gum and sycamores outside my window. Thunderheads are moving in from the west out toward Kansas City and the plains. I'm worrying about buying my first house, making the right choice; I'm weighing the psychic potential of my imminent visit to the volcano and rain forests near where I was born; and I'm trying through all of this to reassure myself on the rightfulness of my place in the university and on this earth. I stretch because my back is stiff, leaning against the maple chair. I've only written about one poem, but it's a kind of casually monumental one that seems to bear well its numerous inscriptions and the intermittent but faithful return of one of its readers. I decide I'm not far from the twenty-year-old who admired Olson's "Maximus, to himself"—I'm still meditating about the uses of knowledge and my own past, writing to revive my faith in the contemplative act as providing some kind of compass for navigating toward this teeming future.

Works Cited

1. I refer to Ezra Pound's translation of "The Seafarer," which he included in his original edition of *Cathay*. I see a relation, here, and in "Canto I" and the "Pisan Cantos," with confession and epic voyaging being the shared acts.

2. Augustine, *The Confessions*, translated by R. S. Pine-Coffin (London: Penguin, 1961). See especially the incident of his robbing the pear tree in Book II.

3. Aristotle, *The Poetics*. I'm referring here especially to Book IX, the section where Aristotle discusses narrative probability and necessity.

4. Charles Olson, *The Maximus Poems* (New York: Jargon/Corinth Books, 1960).

5. A term I borrow from method acting, explained as the main motivational line of a play as discussed in various acting primers and guides by Constantin Stanislavsky (*An Actor Prepares*), Richard Boleslavsky (*Acting: The First Six Lessons*), and others.

6. See Edward Conze's *Buddhism: Its Essence and Development* (New York: Harper-Torchbooks, 2001), for a discussion of these terms. Also his *Buddhist Meditation* (London: Allen Unwin, 1972).

7. Aristotle, *The Poetics*.

8. Augustine, *The Confessions*. See the meditation on time in Book XI.

9. See Robert Brower and Earl Miner's *Japanese Court Poetry* (Stanford: Stanford University Press, 1961) for discussions of these terms in relation to the classical tradition of Japanese poetry.

10. I paraphrase from several of Winters's remarks throughout the critical *oeuvre*, but perhaps the most well-known comments occur near the end of "The Morality of Poetry" from *Primitivism and Decadence*, later reprinted in the justifiably famous *In Defense of Reason* (Athens, Ohio: Swallow Press, 1947).

On Walt Whitman's *Leaves of Grass*

The summer of '73, I was on my way to Japan after graduating from college in California. I won a fellowship sweepstakes of sorts, one of the 70 graduates from 35 colleges across the country who'd been tapped for a swank nonacademic fellowship. What were my plans? "To fuck around and write for a year in Japan," I said, smugly hip. I'd never been nor had anyone in my family been back in the hundred or so years we'd been Americans.

Bert Meyers, the Los Angeles poet who was my first poetry teacher, had constantly and consistently mentioned several great poets to me. Although my own tastes had run to Pablo Neruda, Gary Snyder, Philip Levine, and whosoever might have been on the cover of "The Rolling Poem"—the *American Poetry Review*—Bert had enjoined me to make studies of Yeats, Charles Baudelaire, Emily Dickinson, and Walt Whitman above all. And all were mysteries to me—I'd managed to read none of them during an entire undergraduate curriculum of English Literature and Far Eastern Studies. I'd traded an education in nineteenth-century American literature for Japanese and Chinese literature in translation, for T'ang Dynasty Chinese poetry and painting. I'd given up a semester of Yeats—something I'd planned and wished for—and instead shored up some German and social sciences in order to graduate. I'd done myself in with choices, lower division electives, and courses not taken.

So I was reading Whitman the summer after Commencement, driving around my little L.A. suburban hometown from drive-in to Chinese take-out to the branch of Sumitomo Bank that would receive my fellowship check in America and dispense cash to me in Shibuya, Japan. I had a shitty Signet edition, a "pocket" Whitman, with a hard-glue spine and a cartoon cover that made our poet of the open road look something like a Musketeer from a Hollywood costume drama. It was hard to get into the stuff, frankly. I mean, the spiritual claims, the grandiose rhetoric, its speechifying. I'd glance through the poems, trying to imagine an audible lyric voice for them, and it was impossible. I preferred Georg Trakl, Attila József, Han Shan in translation.

I had no "training" in Whitman, but only Bert's praise for him to guide me. Bert had said Whitman was "the poet of American spiritual optimism, *before* America had turned to shit." I remembered snatches of classroom commentary about Whitman other English majors—distant cousins to me by my senior year—had mentioned over dorm dining hall dinners. Democracy. Barbaric yawp. Indian religions. Hegelian *Spirit.* Driving Redondo Beach Boulevard in a Chevy Nova, negotiating highway dividers and islands and left-turn signals and merging traffic, I asked myself, "What the fuck does all *that* mean?"

"Spontaneous me," "My limbs, my veins dilate," "I am the poet of the Body and I am the poet of the Soul," and "I depart as air" were all lines that cracked me up. Knowing derivation and influence doesn't work in reverse, I still caught a whiff of Bob Dylan in the line about "boot-soles." When the poet yelled about having a feeling in his big toe, I thought of Stevie Wonder. Simplicity. Directness. Bold speech. And no cunning.

Whitman was sailing by me and I was sailing by him. He meant a corny book stuffed into the back pocket of my Levi's. He meant a conversation I couldn't get into, another of my teacher's "greats" who eluded me. "Not my *thang*," I excused myself. And I planned to forget him.

On the way to the beach one night, driving around L.A. to console myself with the dark emptiness that sand and ocean could give, without my girlfriend who had moved with her family north to a coastal town upstate, I switched on the car radio. I was driving my father's car—the one he'd given me so that I could sell it, so that I could go to college. The one he'd bought back from me once he'd given it. A BMW, it had FM capability. I punched the tuning button to a station my father liked. Jazz. K-GO, it's called today; its call letters were then something else.

Drums: *Booom. Shboom. Whatchaw. Whatchatchatat.*
Chacaww. Whatchatchatchat. Chacaww.
Piano: *Boomph, boomph, boomph, a-boomph, bawum, baww.*
Silence.
Boomph, boomph, booph, a-boomph, bawum, BAWW. Silence.
Cha-boom, boom, boom. Silence.
Cha-boom, boom, boom. Silence.
Tenor: *Bwee-daaah, daaah.*
Bweeup-daaah, daaaah. Bweeup.
Daaah, daaah.
Bweeup, daaah, daaah.
Dwee, dah-dah, daaah, daaah, bweeup, daaah, daaah.
Bass: *Boomphum-Boom*
Bwaawhoom.
Boomphum-Boom
Bwaawhoom.

It was "Equinox" by John Coltrane. Near the beginning of his "modal" period. He took a simple tune, a melodic line, and gave it a bit of syncopation. Then he repeated it. Again and again. The "head," it was called. A "vamp," my musician friends called it. "My Favorite Things" was elaborate compared with this. "Equinox" was a chattery drum, traps and cymbals; a presto piano vamp; then a reverberating bass plucking out an ostinato, vaguely reminiscent of bluesy, big-band Mingus except it was made minimal. Well, basic. Nuttin dere *but* da bass. *Paah-doom, doom-doom.* Vibration. *Paah-doom, doom-doom.* Vibration.

Then Coltrane's tenor line. A rip. *Bwee-daaah, daaah.* On the Selmer. Big, bell-like notes over the buoyant bass. From the grave, man, as Coltrane had kicked the night of the Newark Riots in '67, and this was '73. Big noise. Simple noise. And it was beautiful. Like a work song. Like a chorus of angels made to do the work of man. Fucking *American* music.

It had the beauty of the spoken word. Like a verse from Psalms or Lamentations. I heard in it the dithyrambs of Ecclesiastes. "Listen to the Preacher," I told myself, "for he *hath* the Word of God." The Coltrane tune proceeded like anaphoric verse. It set up a rhythm. It used a phrase that it repeated. Again and again. And then it made it change. It made variations that spun and twisted back on themselves, but always returned in some way to the first phrase. If it made crescendo, there would again be a crescendo in the line or two down. Or it would have decrescendo—the opposite. If an accelerando beginning, an accelerando ending somewhere else. A kind of speech. *Phrase. Repeat. Repeat. Variation. Super variation. Return phrase.* A sequence something like free-verse poetry.

Walt Whitman's poetry. For Coltrane had given to music the prosodic and emotional secret of Whitman. And through Coltrane I *learned* to hear Whitman, finally. I carried Whitman throughout Japan. Throughout the sojourn year in Japan, walking Bashō's narrow road, visiting temples, partying with a six-foot Australian disco women, sneaking out of the monastery, and practicing my poet's identity in a triply funktified collision of cultures that was my soul, I carried *Leaves of Grass* around with me like the bass-bottom of a melody, like 'Trane's tenor line set to the rhythms of my step. I had a kosmos in my big toe, Jack.

Three years later, in Seattle, working on a poem in the parlor room of my apartment in the University district, I was playing a tape of Coltrane's "Equinox" on my Sony cassette player. I was trying to write a poem about the open road, about Highway 99 in California. About taking some kind of car trip like that asshole Jack Kerouac celebrated in *On the Road.* I wanted a rhythm. I wanted a compositional structure. I wanted a musical rhetoric of form.

Boomp-boomph shBWOOM BWOOM BOOM!
Bwee-daaah, daaah.

I felt Coltrane in me then. I felt his phrases. An upswelling of music like sexual potency. I heard Whitman. Whitman's "Starting from Paumanok." The barbaric yawp fit like Coltrane's saxophone over Paul Chambers's bassline. You try it sometime. It's the same. You may surge with the ocean of life. You may surge with American music.

If you ask me again, I'd say Whitman means Coltrane to me, that Coltrane means Whitman. Nineteenth-century optimistic ofay runs into twentieth-century reformed drug-addict cool Negro saxophone genius. They depart as air. Look for them under the bassline. Of all our voices they are with us, camaradoes. Step and toe. *Bweeup.*

The Academy Reading Series
Featured Poet
R. S. Thomas

The work of R. S. Thomas, Welsh poet and Anglican minister, born in 1913 and, therefore, like his American contemporary Kenneth Rexroth, a bit of a throwback to pre-Modern standards and sensibilities, was first introduced to me by my teacher, the late Bert Meyers. I had just returned to Los Angeles from Japan at the time and was on my way to Michigan for graduate school. I had only meant to phone Bert before I got on the plane to Detroit the next day. But Bert had not accepted my excuses, would not allow me to beg off a visit, and had shamed me into making the long, hot drive to his house in Claremont by talking about how it was known that the T'ang poets of China would ride six days on horseback and mule just to read each other their new work. He knew well my love for Chinese poetry and my desire for a sense of tradition and continuity in my life. He also knew how to appeal to my sense of guilt and challenge. "So, my young friend, if Tu Fu can ride a leaky junk down the Yellow River to pay his respects to Li Po, and if Johann Bach could walk over a hundred miles on his Easter vacation to knock on the door and introduce himself to Buxtehude, then surely a Japanese American like you can drive a Chevy through mere smog and heavy traffic to see a poor and lonely Jew." Bert was right. I owed him homage and still needed to be taught something.

What he taught me was the poetry of R. S. Thomas. When I arrived in the midafternoon, Bert answered the door and immediately sat me down at the dining table where he normally faced me for these sessions. He pushed a stack of books toward me, which fanned out across the table like a deck of outsized cards.

"You see these books?" he asked. "These are the best books of poetry I've read in English in a long time. They are so good I almost can't believe anyone who is an Anglo composing in English wrote them." He raised himself so he was sitting erect. "They should have been written by a Spaniard, or an Arab, or a Turk, or maybe one of your holy Japanese country Buddhists. Somebody who understands beauty *and* oppression, somebody with heart, with a gifted tongue, and a good deal of wise doubt. It should have been a Jew!" Bert rose from his seat and stamped his foot for emphasis. "Except he has too little irony!" he shouted.

Since I neither laughed nor appeared appropriately shocked for his satisfaction, Bert raised a forefinger into the air, the way the Buddha is said to have done at birth, proclaiming himself the world-honored one, and grabbed one of the books. I remember how blue its covering was, how handsomely it was bound with a rounded spine, and how, compared to American books, it was just undersize. "Listen to this, Garrett," he demanded, "and you might become almost as wise as a Jew—or, in this case, a *Welshman*!" And he laughed that needling giggle, his teeth clamped over his tongue, eyes fixed on me to see if he'd accomplished the effect he wanted. He had. I was listening as if I were Ananda.

Bert read a short poem out loud and praised it for its music, its cadence, its control of tone and its focus of emotion. Then he read another, praising its form and spare but expert use of rhyme. "This is a poet who understands tragedy," he said, "who understands loss and living through it without bitterness, without stridency and self-proclaimed high school tough-guy heroics." Bert was speaking against some of my infatuations and some of my worries. He knew I cared about real political issues and wanted literature to address them, wanted that my own poetry should be able to address them. He also knew I sought a poetry of history. And, I'm guessing, now some fifteen years after this meeting, he thought he'd found it for me. He gave me a great gift, and he underscored it with his own authority as my teacher and his own conviction as a poet.

"I hear Yeats here," Bert said. "This R. S. Thomas has appreciated and studied Yeats well, internalized and simplified, to his own rural and Welsh purposes, the Yeatsian sense of cadence and rhythm and modulated stresses, the Irishman's sense of diction and emotional decorum. And, with Yeats, he shares a sense of cultural patriotism and a sometime visionary's conviction in the poetic pursuit. I hear too a rejection of Auden and his discursive drivel—it's obvious. And I hear someone who is used to the loving ring of speech—it makes sense he's a minister—familiar as he is, like your Miyazawa Kenji, with the plough and the sufferings of the poor. He's someone who depends as much on neighbors for news—*people!*—as he does on newspapers or TV or instructions from the military. And he loves *two* languages—the English he lives and writes in and the Gaelic of his ancestors. So he lives in two languages, two cultures, maybe two distinctly different if not warring faiths. I can't believe he's as committed an Anglican as Eliot, for example. And my favorite religious poems of his are the ones which are full of doubt and pessimism—like the prose of Melville and Hawthorne, so much more interesting than the juvenile faith of the Beats nowadays."

Bert said a lot more about Thomas, and he read aloud poem after poem until it was time for dinner. I think this was a particularly special lesson for me because Bert had found in Thomas a poet who lived in modernity and not in retreat from it, who saw himself as a member of a conquered or colonized race of people, yet who was able to write, out of that acute self-awareness, a speakable poetry of wisdom and dignity. Thomas's poetry is aggrieved in tone, but beautiful to hear and to recite. And he seemed an interesting example for me personally.

From hunting in the English reference guide *Contemporary Poets*, I found out the bare facts about Thomas's life. He was born in Cardiff, Glamorgan, in Wales on March 29, 1913. He was educated at University College in Bangor and at St. Michael's College at the University of Wales, receiving a B.A. in Classics in 1935. In 1940, he married Mildred Eldridge. Thereafter, I read a dizzying chronicle of his clerical appointments, most of them at posts that sounded as magical and faraway as the names of my own Hawaiian places might seem to a native of Wales. Thomas was ordained a deacon in 1936 and priest the following year. He served as curate of Chirk and of Hanmer, rector of Manafon, vicar of St. Michael's Eglwysfach and of St. Hywyn, Aberdaron with St. Mary, Bodferin. As far as I could tell then, and so far as I know now, he lives with his wife at Sam-y-Plas, Y Rhiw, Pwllheli, Gwynedd nearby his latest post where he served as rector of Rhiw.

During this life of service to his church, Thomas has managed to keep his art alive as well, publishing some twenty books of poetry, which range across the years from his first collection called *The Stones of the Field* from Druid Press in 1946 to his most recent volume entitled *Later Poems: A Selection* from Macmillan in 1983. He has done his craft and his tradition a good deal of good, not only as a practitioner but as an editor as well, having compiled critical anthologies of George Herbert, Wordsworth, and Edward Thomas. He has also collected anthologies of country and religious verse and authored a volume of occasional prose. And distinctions have come—his work receiving the Heinemann Award, the Queen's Gold Medal for Poetry, the Welsh Arts Council Award, and, most recently, the Cholmondeley Award. From simply scanning his life in profile, it seems the dutiful and devout one anyone might expect from reading the poetry.

Indeed, the facts underscore what the poetry seems to say— that Thomas's is a life rooted in consistent devotion to the tasks of the poet and that of the minister. I certainly agree with the English critic Stan Smith when he writes that "R.S. Thomas's calling is pastoral in a double sense, as a minister in the Welsh hill-country concerned with the spiritual salvation of his parishioners, and as a poet preoccupied with their figurative redemption in verse." Smith characterizes the work as "pastoral poetry with a sour edge to it, set in a bleak, eroded landscape." Though I myself see as much beauty as erosion in Thomas's countryside, this "sour edge" of mood mixed with the redemptive urge is what finally sustains my attraction to Thomas's poetry. It cannot simply be enough to admire his fine technical skills or even his courage of sentiment. What truly inspires is his acute concern for a ravaged place and for the confused but passionate remnant of folk in that place. Though I wonder about this now, I often thought then that, particularly in my reading of his early work, he saw himself as almost a Welshman first and a minister only second, and *that* was compelling to me. For a poet to be loyal to a place and a people before he was loyal to a "role" seemed astonishingly authentic to me. I wanted a bit of that for myself, of course, to be loyal to my own beginnings in Hawai'i and yet to write a poetry that wasn't simply a poetry of pastoral retreat. Thomas had already accomplished that.

I perceived that he wrote out of a feeling not only for the considerable beauties of the Welsh landscape, but also out of a sense of its exploitation by tourism and the need to correct the misperception of this economically oppressed region as simply "picturesque." It was apparent he possessed a sense of tradition and traditional life—farming and all its chores, the self-reliant and post-Neolithic technologies of rural survival, etc.—yet he chose not to romanticize them but rather to use them as a backdrop for his critique of the economic deprivation and emotional paucity of that existence. It was significant to me, in reading poem after poem describing the landscape and characterizing the people, that Thomas wrote almost as much out of a charitable scorn as out of any nostalgia. That all of this was set in the near-magical scenes of dense fogs and emerald hillsides of Wales made the work that much more pertinent to me as someone born in the Hawaiian rain forest—another landscape wrapped in clouds and in the torn rags of rural poverty. I don't know if I'd ever have been able to write about my own natal places with much passion and critical acid without the example of R. S. Thomas.

Thomas's sense that his was an almost marginalized homeland—and Wales does seem, indeed, to be as much that for him as Martinique might have been, for all his idealizations, quite compromised for Aimé Césaire—was joined to a feeling for his people that was at once critical and affectionate. Many of his early poems are portraits of the Welsh "peasantry," exposing their despair and cultural limitations at the same time as they acknowledge their toughness and self-mockery. If John Millington Synge's Aran islanders were bewildered by the encroachment of modernity into their seafaring lives, then Thomas's Welsh shepherds and farmers, some fifty years later, are beleaguered and all but displaced by it. The tenor of the emotions Thomas found in his people helped me clarify my own sense of the emotions of mine—working his poor harvest, a Welshman portrayed in "A Welshman to Any Tourist" seems to articulate the mixed helplessness and resentment the underclass in Hawai'i feels toward our own visitors—we do need them, and yet . . . they shame us with their wealth and the way they seem to take an easier pleasure out of their lives. Our joys are aggrieved, and yet, like anyone, we love our particular place on earth.

In Spanish, there seem to be words and phrases, respectable ones about respectable feelings, that articulate this special sensibility and dangerous political position with dignity, amplitude, and a paradoxical restraint. Sentiments like these are often decried in English, associated as they are with jingoism, anticolonialism, false and marginalized loyalties, and a romanticized ethnic pride. Yet, phrases like *la gente* and *mi patria* and a chant like "El pueblo unido, jamás será vencido" have their place in my heart and in the hearts of others I love and admire. In 1973, Victor Jara of Chile said words like these as he led, in a final and completely fatal songfest, the crowd detained in the Santiago soccer stadium. And French too has been seized as an international yet appropriately local language. When I read Césaire's poem *Cahier d'un retour au pays natal*, I admit that a special kind of recognition flares in my soul. And what they all understood is something Thomas also understands, and yet he has carried his own loyalty elsewhere and made a further point—that the spiritual love for a place might best be served by being transformed into a love for a spiritual place. That, at bottom, what we love is that upwelling of the soul itself and not so much whatever has been its tangible inspiration. The spirit—like Wales or Hawai'i—is also a country. Nowhere in English contemporary verse is a sense of this clearer or quietly ferocious than in the poetry of R. S. Thomas.

From "A Poet's Notebook"

These journal pages emerged out of a time when I was "between books"—*Yellow Light* and *The River of Heaven*. I began it while working on a PhD in critical theory, then kept it through my first academic jobs—first as a visitor at USC and then at UC Irvine, next as an assistant professor at the University of Missouri. I felt even more then that I was an outsider than I do now. My constant company of white professors and students assumed that cultural identities were all fixed and solved, or that they were at the very least not a concern of anyone "serious." I wasn't having the close conversations with people about politics, literature, and ethnicity that I craved. This social and professional life offended me, yet I could not complain. By then, I had decided *against* a simple cultural nationalism—writing my first book of poems persuaded me out of that—yet I wished not to work toward any kind of "assimilationist" or "closet-ethnic" aesthetic either. I wanted to be *rooted*, I wanted to think my way toward a considered aesthetic and political position regarding my passion to create compatible poetic, regional, and ethnic identities. These journal pages helped me do that. I put together much of the aesthetic that resulted in *The River of Heaven*—a book poised between Hawai'i and Los Angeles, attempting to occupy the silence between cultural centrism and the realities of diaspora. Yeats's *Autobiography* and Allan Seager's biography of Theodore Roethke, *The Glass House*, were inspirations regarding these kinds of regional and ethnic self-creations. My own journal, then, became an opportunity for fulminating these kinds of issues. It was an affair with my own emotions and intellect and a resolute pursuit of an unsanctioned, hidden history. Like poetry, it was a secret place of the heart, a smithy of my soul.

October 1: Balboa. There's something like "imaginative will"—a desire to exercise the mind, to use the imagination, a wish to conjure worlds of one's imagining simply to enjoy the task of that imagining. It's fun to tell stories, so we tell them. Wolf tickets sold not for profit but for the gain of the feelings they inspire.

This is what the theorists mean when they talk about the "repose of the imagination." The self-contemplative ideal that Flaubert is sometimes said to have invented, that Stephen Daedalus endorses and improves upon in *A Portrait of the Artist as a Young Man.*

This is why so many of us prefer to live in these worlds of our own design—the idea of the poetic retreat, "Peter Quince at the Klavier," Kamo-no-Chōmei in his hut ten-foot square, Kenkō in his idleness, and Bashō in his unreal dwelling. I'm told that Pope had a fabulous garden to which he'd retire to write his caustic verse epistles. Whether he really did or not I'm not sure, being no scholar, but I am sure that he had a bower of sorts within the territory of his own poems. It was probably more pleasant for him than society.

The Chinese have a word for poet that means "sorcerer" or "magician," but it also means "hermit." The notion contains within it an idea of the poet as alchemist of the human spirit, poetry as a kind of spiritual pharmaceutical.

But society still remains and does so in the world. What can poems do for them? I'm fairly Confucian about this question and believe that if poems can order our thinking and inspire noble emotions within us, then in doing these things, they indirectly help the world. Poems inspire *jen*, a kind of metaphysical propriety and liberation within us that we need to keep going, maintain a generous-minded social equilibrium that can carry us through most of what's mental and trivial in our daily routines. Like the song says, "You gotta have heart!" and good poems, like good songs, restore that in us, the Japanese say, the life spirit. Love.

But life is so hard here
it has to be carved in a tree.
　　　Lance Patigian

October 8: The world's body has been denied us. I want it back.
And I use the erotic resonance of that metaphor purposefully
because it is precisely that strong physical relationship with the
world that modern, particularly modern urban, life seems to
deny us. Poetry is my way of re-establishing that relationship,
recapturing that lost love. It's a hermeneutic desire.

For Japanese Americans, the past is a corpse, a dead and foul
thing we have all either avoided or been shielded from. Because
of the circumstances of our history and its conjunction with
a perhaps necessarily stoic psychological culture, the past has
been something to be ashamed of and overcome, forgotten. I
want to go into this territory of our dead, make them speak and
reveal to me their emotional lives still unaccounted for. I'd like
to spend my time listening to these ghosts, learning what I can
of the circumstances of their lives—the immigration and early
settlement, WWII and Relocation, the post-war return—and tell
about them in a book of poems.

I propose to enter these lives through the study of documents
and oral histories.

It's my way of bringing back what John Crowe Ransom called
"the world's body."

October 17: What the Derrideans seem to want is the freedom to
read a text in the same way as a poet "reads" the world—for the
play of signifiers it "engenders" in their own texts.

1984

June 23: Eugene. Seems to me the most beautiful, sentimental,
and extravagant of all arts must be the hand-gestures of the
hula . . .

The "Romantic Image" is simply a tool for emotional concentra-
tion and the release of emotion and a more complex imagery

towards the making of a symbolic pattern that *has* emotion in it (i.e., that inspires and not merely "stands for" emotion). Yeats made it a craft and a discipline because of his needs and his background—his aesthetic roots in Pre-Raphaelite painting and an ideal of craftsmanship that must have been born partly out of a nativist pride, partly out of an atavistic affection for things Byzantine—"of hammered gold and gold enameling . . ."

The trick is to make the memory, (or) the *imagined* experience, stronger than anything else in one's consciousness, to make the "pretend game" the one that counts, that is the death trap. Tricks of the mystics and the contemplatives should prove handy: simplify one's life; spend lots of time in solitude; avoid chaotic, undisciplined experiences until one is prepared to encounter them; quell the violent passions (jealousy, envy, malice). I'd add one dictum probably not present in any handbook for contemplatives—cultivate a refined seriousness. Lots of the great and the near-great did this—one has only to think of Monet's gardens at Giverny, Neruda's study full of varicolored, beach-scavenged bottles, ships-in-bottles, conch shells, and that sea siren Madonna he scrounged and subsequently enshrined near his desk. Wordsworth had the entire Wye Valley, Frost his New Hampshire farm, Jeffers Tor House, Yeats his tower in Ballylee.

One of my most profound regrets is that I don't have a proper portrait of my father. I wonder—could I get a snapshot somehow and ask Wakako to paint one for my study?

Or could I imagine one myself? Paint it, "with poetry" as it were?

I remember a service picture, not a formal one, but a studio group portrait of three G.I.s in uniform, one of them my father. I seem to remember they had leis and big grins on, a stripe or two each, and service decorations. And except for being sepia-toned, the print was untinted.

What was lost?—those sparkling moments of clear emotion and generousness in the past, heirlooms of consciousness.

Returning vets, conquering heroes, 18 or 19 years old . . .

Worry is a mental erosion, a disease like leprosy upon consciousness, contagious and ultimately, to the imagination, fatal.

1985

January 14: Columbia. Reading Robert Morgan's poems, I realize that my instincts are quite conservative in terms of poetic value—

> richness of diction and imagery
> strong, straight } crafted narrative
> a vanished thing set down in
>   language the goal—this
>   seems Frostian somehow,
>   perhaps Yankee,
>   though I can call up similarities to Japanese & Chinese
>   poetry—
>   Tsurayuki's *Preface*
>   T'ao Ch'ien's poems for wine &
>   friendship

My early teachers were conservative too in terms of their literary values—Bert Meyers, Stanley Crouch, and John Haines. They wanted fairly straightforward and simplified diction, an elegance or stateliness of *tone*, and startling or even sometimes dazzling imagery and metaphor. Ideas were restricted to the aesthetic or the chthonic, a certain kind of primitivism the force behind much of this, with radical politics thrown in as spice, conscience, and Utopian dream.

Coherence, literary and political and emotional, was above all the guiding principle—a hatred of cultural and spiritual atavism.

Derrida in his critique of Kant and Hegel attacks this as a desire for religion, their philosophies a kind of secular theology smuggling back deism in what purports to be a rational philosophy, irrational desire masquerading in the rhetorical robes of dialectical reason.

Poetry, for my teachers, conducted no such masquerade. Rather, it declared itself as heir to the role religion might have served in more coherent societies, ritual might have performed in primitive cultures.

June 27: Volcano. I guess it's true—my problem is a chronic one, that consciously and unconsciously *I make myself cultureless because of an internalized oppression.* I try to fit in with my surroundings to the point that I repress the better nature within, eliminate the Hawaiian, ghetto L.A., and Japanese roots.

There is nobility in these ways, there is a good and strong side to these impulses I should try to learn to tap into and restore so that I can maintain myself better as a healthy and creative psyche.

Here in Volcano, I feel like I've found the real thing again, found my *own way* and I'm not so worried about being competitive so long as I can always come from myself, so long as the poems can come from that better part of me so I breathe easy when I write, reach out to all the best parts of memory and imagination.

July 6: Kawela. C. says that what I *wish* I could be is a "folk" artist the way Alan Lau is or say, someone actually indigenous. But the reality is I can't be that since I don't come out of an intact, received tradition but needed to construct my own art, amalgamating elements and influences eclectically, choosing and absorbing from pop culture, high art and literature, and a smattering of learning in Oriental studies. Not even the folklorist that Yeats or Synge was, the scholar that Snyder and Merwin are, I've had to freeboot, wildcat, and jerry-rig my practice together as Simon Rodia did his towers, Mingus did his music.

Writerly riches are like vast landholdings—rent comes in from everywhere and you can inhabit what parcels you choose, when you choose. If you have a village, a kingdom, that you write from and about, you are wealthy to the point of embarrassment. *Material.* Rich in material. Faulkner, Garcia Marquez, Hardy.

[I write this 500 yds. from where my Kubota grandfather died in a state nursing home on Kamehameha Highway. I write this 2 miles from the sugar mill, surrounded by canefields where two generations of my family worked as laborers, where they owned nothing, not even the shacks they lived in.]

August 6: Eugene. Poetry is a funny, appealing life. What it does I think is allow me to try to live as rich an emotion life as I can, mark passing events with a few words of the proper solemnity, speak as if I were writing letters to home to someone like my wife. Poetry ritualizes the emotions, makes, in the words of Grotowski, a kind of poor theater out of them, gives them a small public spectacle so that they can appear and be honored.

The Activity of the Poet

> The poet lives in a world whose newspapers and maga-
> zines and books and motion pictures and radio stations
> and television stations have destroyed, in a great many
> people, even the capacity for understanding real poetry,
> real art of any kind.
>
> —Randall Jarrell, "The Obscurity of the Poet"

I'm looking from the quiet window of my study at the honey
locust and maple trees leafing out in the front yard. It's mid-
April and Missouri's under a cold, navy-gray sky. A bird I don't
yet know the name of assembles its nest in the rain gutter of my
house, and the intermittent thrash of passing cars and metallic
rumble of big interstate rigs carry from the freeway six blocks
down. It's a suburbanish street out there, desolate now except
for my gaze peopling the emptiness with the willed tricks of
memory and the insinuations of my daydreaming. In the kitch-
en, through the shut door of my study, I can hear my nineteen-
month-old son singing himself asleep for his morning nap; the
wood floors creak as Ran, his Korean babysitter, walks him to
and fro. I see a brown cardinal swoop from the sycamores in the
ravine across the street, glide over my front yard, and disappear
over the black roof of the garage. The quiet now filling up the
house tells me Alexander is asleep, and I might have two hours
to get some of this told.

In the eighties, as in other times, there are innumerable plea-
surable distractions and vexing concerns to command the atten-
tion of the middle class—professional sports or the out-of-town
ballet in for a special performance, news headlines and bills to
pay, home computers and the WordStar program to learn, a sag-

ging roof or noisy muffler to fix, a new lover or home video—all of which conspire to consume any leisure of the mind, particularly that of the mind engaging its own history. And producing out of that engagement a version of the self and human experience distinct from any other version in the available culture.

I'm talking, of course, about the special case of poetry, and defining it here as an act not only of writing in meter or some other kind of form, but as an act of contemplation, a consideration of the past and one's personal derivation from it, an act, in fact, of self-discovery and origination. This, for me, is the primary activity of the poet—an act of geomancy in the primitive sense, not so much a *foretelling* (although this *always* happens, if only as a by-product), but a *placement* in relationship to the past and, by extension, to the future as well, a resituating of the self in balance with its past character and significant events. It's the kind of placement that was *sacred* in previous times, similar to the surveys of Oriental magicians before a city or a temple was built, the polar-axial layouts of Chang-an and Nara, and all their multitudes of pavilions and Buddhist halls. It is, as Pound or Confucius would say, metaphysical and moralistic both at once, "keeping the rites."

In this advanced time, with the proliferation of information systems and the concurrent displacement of the written word by the visual image as the main vehicle for not only mass communication but mass culture as well, when even information risks becoming invaluable private property in the working economy and the myth of science as key to human emancipation has all but usurped religious and humanistic traditions as the central narrative schema of our culture; the poet today might therefore seem a frail, superfluous figure, even more useless than the blind and breasted man, aged and stinking from a score of open wounds, chattering nervous warnings and long elegantly phrased but indulgent speeches to himself in the vacant lots and the outskirts of Thebes. He is, at best, perhaps to be pitied for his dementia, and, at worst, to be condemned for irrelevance and nonproductivity. Certainly, his use is difficult, if not impossible to see, and he does seem a nuisance slowing others in their daily rounds.

But the poet today is not so frequently the derelict Tiresias I have described above, repellent and prophetic, banished from the Republic, since he or she may be a person like me, a university professor and head-of-household, properly credentialed with advanced degrees and a public style, somewhat abashed to be justifying himself and his role in society. So it is at least with all the poets I'll speak about here, taking their places as educators within our society, teachers of a craft and purveyors of a limited, ostensibly arcane tradition. As we prepare for classes or stroll down a hallway headed toward our committee meetings, we perhaps carry this Tiresias around as our myth, his role and his story a reminder of our tradition. In a world of mass media and mass culture, in an economy of consumables and disposables, we teach something about the survival of the private self, and we praise memory.

Greg Pape has a poem in *Border Crossings*, his first book, in which he reconstructs a complicated incident from his youth, an event of transformative conciliation, and, in a real sense, the true birth of his family. It's called "My Happiness":

> That spring day
> I stood in the new grass
> and watched the man cutting steel
> with an arc welder—
> the man my mother had just married.
> I watched as he leaned in his welder's mask
> and held a blue-white star
> to a steel rod until it was glowing with heat.
> A cloud drifted in front of the sun
> and darkened the land
> the way sweat darkened his back.
> Then with some slip of the body
> or misjudgment of a man
> given over wholly to his work
> a piece of glowing metal
> fell like a tiny meteor into his boot.
> His hand went down
> his fingers seared.
> Then the smell of burnt flesh,
> a groan of pain, and the crazy hopping.
> He fumbled in his pocket for a knife
> slit open the boot and swatted the hot metal
> off his ankle. What could I do?

I ran for mother and a bucket of water.
And that spring day I remember my happiness
as I poured the cold water over his wound
and she put her arm around his neck
and the sun came out
and the mysterious healing began
and he was saying oh jeezus
and she was saying oh honey.

There are so many things going on here—the poet's vivid sense-memory bringing to language the image of the man welding, the "blue-white star" he held, and the meteor falling into his boot; the wonderfully contained story and small cast of characters; even the sly, symbolic patterning of the imagery on sun and cloud, qualities of light and dark—but sweetest of all here is the delight in what is *not* told, but, rather, given to us completely by the situation, the subtleties of the poet's language, and the grand feeling of all of this as recollection.

Pape the poet doesn't call the man his "stepfather," but "the man my mother had just married," giving the strong suggestion of the natural antipathy that existed between the two. Then follows the vivid description of the welding and the accident until we get to the climax of this tiny narrative, when the poet, in the voice of recollection, asks "What could I do?"—"I ran for mother and a bucket of water," he answers, matter-of-factly, and then begins the short, chantlike close of the poem, a paean to memory, love, and the American language.

What's significant to me, finally, is the way all of this story has been told—*skirting* the transformation of voice and consciousness from adult to the child's, avoiding the kind of complete entry into the child's world that a film or more inept narrative strategy might necessitate. The poet keeps a firm hold on his own consciousness and perspective as a poet *recollecting*—he's stepping back some, into his own past, lifting an event from it out of insignificance and anonymity and privileging it by this act of recall, but he doesn't abandon the present, writerly self, the consciousness that, in fact, makes this act of privileging and homage possible in the first place. It's a doubled if not a multiple self we see here, and, thus, a sublime one, made grander for the amplification, made part of that past the poet recalls, those events, and those two lovely, colloquially eloquent people who were his parents. The poet has retrieved a moment of great and intimate familial love and has succeeded in making it feel almost cosmic without obscuring any of its familiarity—a magnificent and subtle accomplishment completely beyond the powers of mass culture and its sentimentalizing.

Sometimes the poet's memory transforms a legion of similar or repeated events into a single image rather than the narrative itself. This, perhaps, is a function of the peculiar, imagistic, and postmodern imagination, yet the process is not so different from the medieval practice (from Dante on) of figuring as complex an idea and set of narratives as God and his Paradise as a roseate chain of concentric and pulsing lights. Regardless, I can think of one poet, a very close contemporary, who's understood and demonstrated this trick of memory and inclination of the mind. His name is Mark Jarman, and the poem is called "The Supremes":

In Ball's Market after surfing till noon,
we stand in wet trunks, shivering
as icing dissolves off our sweet rolls
inside the heat-blued counter oven,
when they appear on his portable TV,
riding a float of chiffon as frothy
as the peeling curl of a wave.
The parade M.C. talks up their hits
and their new houses outside of Detroit
and old Ball clicks his tongue.
Gloved up to their elbows, their hands raised
toward us palm out, they sing,
"Stop! In the Name of Love" and don't stop
but slip into the lower foreground.

Every day of a summer can turn,
from one moment, into a single day.
I saw Diana Ross in her first film
play a brief scene by the Pacific—
and that was the summer it brought back.
Mornings we paddled out, the waves

would be little more than embellishments:
lathework and spun glass,
gray-green with cold, but flawless.
When the sun burned through the light fog,
they would warm and swell,
wind-scaled and ragged,
and radios up and down the beach
would burst on with her voice.

She must remember that summer
somewhat differently, and so must the two
who sang with her in long matching gowns,
standing a step back on her left and right,
as the camera tracked them
into our eyes in Ball's Market.
But what could we know, tanned white boys
wiping sugar and salt from our mouths
and leaning forward to feel their song?
Not much, except to feel it
ravel us up like a wave
in the silk of white water,
simply, sweetly, repeatedly,
and just as quickly let go.
We didn't stop either, which is how
we vanished, too, parting like spray—
Ball's Market, my friends and I.
Dredgers ruined the waves,
those continuous dawn perfections,
and Ball sold high to the high rises
cresting over them. His flight out of L.A.,
heading for Vegas, would have banked
above the wavering lines of surf.
He may have seen them. I have,
leaving again for points north and east,
glancing down as the plane turns.
From that height they still look frail and frozen,
full of simple sweetness and repetition.

Unlike Pape's, Jarman's is a poem of disparate moments, brought together by a flash of insight and the skill of a memory lavish in details and sensuous experience. Several events are recalled here, across distances of time, and the poem shifts focus from one to the other, beginning in the adolescent past of the poet, his days of surfing and then loitering at Ball's Market, moving through the recent experience that brought on all the recalling—seeing Diana Ross playing a scene in her first film— and back again to the same adolescent past before it ends in a moment of speculative resolution to that past narrative, which in turn inspires a veiled confession and assertion about the imagination. This is not, then, a poem of simple recall, but a careful unfurling of the nostalgic impulse, and evocation coupled with a cagey demonstration of the way the poet's mind can fix a whole complex of events into a single, sensuous image.

The wave, "the silk of white water" as Jarman describes it, ravels him up like a song, like the silky Motown voice of Diana Ross, and like the riptide of sexual urge, only faintly resisted, surging through the entire poem. The poet is not the pornographer, however, obsessed with prurience and the infantile. He is rather a technician of the imagination here, multiplying his image and assertions, bringing the wave, the song, his own emerging sexual awareness, and the memories of an entire summer of his life together in the sweet repetitions of froth, those "float[s] of chiffon" to which his poem pays homage. His poem ends, in a marvelously Romantic and yet contemporary gesture of surmise—one that Coleridge might have made had he been robust, allowed to surf, and fortunate enough to have listened to the Supremes—guessing that Ball, after selling "high to the high rises," might have glanced back "above the wavering lines of surf" as his plane, heading for a new life in Vegas—that inevitable city—banked above the City of Angels. A fitting enough close, but the poem goes on, delivering the poet's testimony of his own witnessing, seeing those same waves as he glances down from one of his own repeated departures—a doubled image, wavelike, of Ball's leave-taking—and notices "how frail and frozen" they were, almost like a fond memory, "full of simple sweetness and repetition." As much as anything else, "The Supremes" is, in Wallace Stevens's phrase, a poem of the act of the mind.

But let me amend, or tie an addendum onto, Stevens's criterion for poetry—it is, for me, the act of the mind *in contemplation* that is essential. I add the phrase, probably redundant for someone like Stevens or many of his High Modernist contemporaries, because, in our day, the model for mental activity is no longer the philosopher meditating on the worth of recent contributions to civilized learning, nor even the lighthearted aesthetician in reverie over some foppish French thingamajig, but rather—any television commercial, splashy ad in Fortune, or even a spy thriller will demonstrate this—the model is now the embattled professional engaged slightly above his or her capacity and who, by showering or making morning coffee or performing some other routine activity in the plush, nurturing circumstances of a splendidly furnished penthouse or lodge retreat, suddenly is blessed with a flash of insight and rushes hell-bent for the phone, in possession not only of the slick solution to a knotty systems problem, but also of the admiration of board chairmen and, by extension, of American corporate prestige as well. This is the *action* individual, the hero as yuppie Beowulf slaying the corporate Grendel, not much different from the naive victim of the various thriller plots turned redoubtable double-agent, adding up the ploys and deceptions of his pursuers, scheming his homemade counterattack. It is a model of thought that first analyzes and then dictates aggressive action, the American practical sense applied to worldly, ultimately quotidian concerns, the material reward involved notwithstanding. The spy stuff merely glamorizes and makes epic a fairly mundane process. The TV ad-drama makes it *cool* and filthy with money.

What interests me, however, and what, I'm arguing, interests the poet—in the eighties as in any time (if I, like Tu Fu, may be allowed to speak as if I were a man of seventy while still in my thirties)—is *impractical* thought, *pure reason* as Immanuel Kant defines it for us in the dense pages of the great book he wrote those mornings in his cramped, canal apartment after long nights strolling the foggy, cobbled streets of eighteenth-century Amsterdam. It is the mind, in a way, engaged with itself, a primitive, narcissistic activity, somewhat of a mystery and completely without practical value, though its process, for practitioners, has been beneficial for its therapeutic, civilizing qualities. And let me add that it is also a unique, almost spiritual pleasure, not quite so arcane as its false teachers might lead you to believe. The job is to distinguish memory from mere impression, passionate obsession from trivial perversion. This is not always easy to do since the world upholds the latter items in the pairs in order to get its work done, the pushing along of small things, the repression of desire in favor of necessity, fostering "attachment" (*samsara*, in Buddhist terms), and ignoring sentience.

Let me turn, now, to the example of another fine teacher, a poet of dispossession and privation, blessed with a soft, country heart and the kind of understated, quiet expansiveness of vision that is appropriate for one who seems to me a true, familiar child of Walt Whitman. He is Arthur Smith, a man as plainspoken as his name, heir to a line of West Virginia coal miners and migrant croppers in California's Central Valley—the site of that great John Steinbeck novel Arthur's people could have been the model for. His poem is called "Hurricane Warning" and is about self-forgiveness, memory, and consolation. Its occasion is the poet's telling of a photograph he still has of his first wife, deceased for some years now after a tragic, lingering illness. Yet, he doesn't give a long description of her death, nor does he complain about his loss or indulge in any bitterness. He instead invokes a marvelously ornate memory, draws, in his finely wrought phrasings and casually imagistic diction, a picture of an idle moment they once shared, gazing at a field of poppies.

I still have, somewhere,
A photograph of her
        and me leaning out over a balcony railing,
Behind us, I remember, the bay windows
wickered with tape

And the sky spanned
By a single cloud, its underbelly, here and there, smeared
        with that blood-orange hue
We once saw a field of poppies take on

Just before dusk, in the foothills
South of Sonora. There were always poppies, it seemed,
        washing up and dwindling to a golden point on a
            hillside
Otherwise green
        with wild-oats and weeds,

Or tawny with them, depending. I don't know
        what might have become of us in time—ten years,
            twenty
The two of us walking off, as lovers
Are supposed to, hand in hand,

Toward one inevitability
        or another—but time would have had a chance
To deal with us, in its own sweet time.
It would have brought us pain,
        and lulled

It all away; it would have made the hillsides
And the swaths of poppies
        fronting as crops of sunlight
All the more difficult, in the end, to leave;
        and toward the end, it may have left
Us both alone. Along the country backroads,
Wildflowers luxuriate and strive—snowbells, and buttercups,
And the shooting stars that briefly fan
        their faces to the sun.

You can pull over almost
        anywhere you want, and wander,
And lie back in whatever blossoms you can find.
All around you the hills, like sea swells,
        are rolling in

Or rolling out,
        and the clouds you're gazing at
The same, and there seems to be no end of it, no point
        of reference, or anchor,
Except for the faintly bitter scent of the wildflowers
        you chose to walk through, and lie down in.

From a memory of the photograph and its scene, to the sky and
the single cloud, to the color of the cloud finally likened to that
"blood-orange hue" taken on, just before dusk, by a field of pop-
pies, the poet's imagination moves by swift, deft, and affection-
ate associations, recalling the specific—balcony, tape, foothills
south of Sonora—before it generalizes the one scene into a

complex memory of several like scenes, fields of poppies in the plural, enlarging not only the physical, but the emotional scope of the poem as well, opening it up to commentary and speculation about a future to his specific, tragic past that could not have happened, but, in the mental world of this poem, can and does indeed, before the poet retrieves it all back into the beautiful physical projection of lying down in a field luxuriant with wildflowers. He imagines, had his wife lived, that they'd have had their time and, as he says, walked off toward "one inevitability / or another," how it would have brought them pain "and lulled / It all away"—in other words, how they might have led lives of plain, heroic beauty, perhaps even, in the end, alone—a hint, I'm guessing, of some other, less final, separation. Smith does not sentimentalize nor give in entirely passively to his musings—faint wishes—nor accord them any false, added rhetorical pomp. Rather, he speaks almost as if purified from pain and illusion, not quite stern, but honest and clear-eyed, sober as a Henry Fonda or a Jimmy Stewart in any exemplary movie of the thirties. Maturity is what I'm praising here—emotional and psychological—maturity and its consequent self- (and worldly) acceptance.

As I mentioned above, "Hurricane Warning" ends with a wonderfully elegant take-down of physical projection, the poet almost imploring the reader and, at least, invoking him, telling about the plentiful fields of wildflowers and how "You can pull over almost / anywhere you want, and wander, / And lie back in whatever blossoms you can find." Smith talks about the hills like sea swells rolling in and out, "the clouds *you're* gazing at / The same . . ." (emphasis mine) and they all become somehow representative of—symbols and natural cathedrals for—a physically opulent and spiritually buoyant infinitude the poet chooses, in his words, "to walk through, and lie down in." The scene, the reader, the widowered poet, and even his wife gone into the everlasting are all apotheosized, raised up as if after a judgment—here, the poet's—and celebrated, fittingly memorialized in the natural world and in the eloquent, country cadences of Arthur Smith.

The entire poem has been a deceptively low-key tracing of an elaborate act of the mind casting back over personal experience,

71

proceeding by swift associations of sense-memory and narrative projection, a seemingly guileless meditation on the meaning of loss and the consequential emotional worth of having to come to terms with that loss. It is a poem of high, solitary imagination distinct from the concerns of petty capitalists and those others who would wish material profit from all acts of the mind. It is contemplative, stately, full of uncommon grace and an earned wisdom proper to its serious subject.

There is a richness here, the mind in a certain state, a cast of thought that stills itself from flitting from errand to duty to vicissitude and, consequently, can look upon the life of the self as a narrative extending two ways—to the past and toward the future—a narrative of order or of disorder sometimes, of continuity or of dissonance, but one that has the power to take in huge swatches of experience and pick out of them the details to illustrate that which is its persistent desire—first of all, its own meditative harmony (from which all discoveries proceed), and next a consolational, perhaps eremitic, solution to whatever problem has been the object of its contemplation: a traumatic event like a loved one's death or the loss of homelands (say, the Palestinian removal or the relocation of Japanese Americans during World War II), or an abstract problem made concrete as in Augustine's meditation on time or on guilt, or the idea of redemption in Stevens's "Sunday Morning." Could this be the "mind of Winter" Stevens wrote about in one of his lyrics? The "cold eye" that Yeats spoke of in "Under Ben Bulben"? I'm guessing so—meaning the mind that reaches back and looks forward with calm, with some detachment. Ritual mind. *Noh*-mind. A kind of clairvoyance.

> "It is difficult
> to get the news from poems
>   yet men die miserably every day
>   for lack
> of what is found there."
> —William Carlos Williams

Sherod Santos, my colleague in Creative Writing at the University of Missouri, has written a stunning poem on this matter of that elusive state of mind, that somewhat privileged reserve of consciousness I've been talking about. It's called "At the All-Clear," and it concerns a memory from childhood about a reprieve from disaster, an event, once considered and rendered poetically, that is ultimately even more astonishing than disaster itself. Its ostensible subject is the aftermath of a hurricane in—the poet tells me—Hawai'i, where he spent some time during his childhood while his father, a Navy pilot, was stationed there during the Korean War.

I think it's about memory too, the way it works, mysteriously, strenuously, protecting us from bitter losses:

That early in the morning
The villa's huts were still
Shuttered with silver,
Although, in the headlights,

A young woman appeared
Through an unhinged door
To be rubbing the night's
Sleep from her eyes.

The Red Cross truck was
Parked and driverless
Beside the Protestant
Church; and all along

The beaches the heaped
Debris of plantain
And carapace, seaweed,
And striped palm fronds

Lay interlapped like
Parquet on the sand.
As our family and
Neighbors came down

From the high ground,
The souring heat unfocused
The flyspecks floating
In on the tide; and the gulls

Which only the day
Before had been blown
Back off the breakers
Now scavenged along

The shore, above
The dead-water outline
Of the pier. For days
To come, there'd be

A shadow out over
The coral shoals, an
Afterimage, a shard of
Bottle glass pressed flat

In the palm. Our bungalow
Seemed to have been
Pulleyed up from a gash
In the ground: earth-

Spattered, prehistoric,
It stood there staggered
On its shaken stilts . . .
And yet how surprised

We were, each momentarily
Caught as if wondering
What to say at having
Found, inside, that nothing

Had changed, that the table
Was still set for an after-
Noon meal, and there
On the stove was a pot

Of red beans, and another
Of salted rice water.
It could've been
One of these places

We'd run across sometimes
In children's stories,

Where the world's familiar,
While remaining the same,

Will suddenly become
What it has never been,
A place you walk
Through as if in dream:

The air barely rippled
The kitchen curtains
While Mother stood
Washing the unused plates,

While the winged ants beat
Against the light and
Dropped their transparent
Wings on the water.

We first get, in mostly three-beat lines of usually five to seven syllables, carefully enjambed when called for by the spill of syntax and the necessary varieties of rhythm, a precise summary description of the seashore and Quonset huts after the storm. All is elegantly phrased, a collection of efficient yet evocative images, attesting to the strangification of a scene, to us and to the poet, already a bit exotic for its tropical location. But clue words like "dead-water outline" and "afterimage" foreshadow something of the central point and demonstration of the poem, premonitions in image and idea of a vacancy reinhabited that is the poem's final (if only phenomenological) event.

For everything inside their battered, staggered bungalow is astonishingly the same as they had left it before the storm—the table still set, food still in its pots on the stove—the way perhaps that the past remains habitable sometimes, no matter how much we've done or changed in the time between its events and when we choose to think of them again, reimagine them. And how we're surprised even how the familiar, which should have become strange, nevertheless remains familiar even though changed by the act of our returning to it, a world, as the poet says, "suddenly become / ...A place you walk / Through as if in dream. ..." It is a past kept mysteriously intact by the mind—childhood, a scene of parting from loved ones, events and places that have marked and stained us and raveled us up in their subdued, unconscious glory—supernaturally vacant as that little town by the seashore full of desolate, silent streets that John Keats told about in his "Ode on a Grecian Urn." It is all an altar readied for sacrifice or for a kind of worship, a place somehow purged of vicissitude and worldly care, though, as I said, somehow still familiar and habitable, albeit potentially perilous for some of us, nevertheless vibrant and alluring with a clarified kind of presence we can all appreciate in our best moments.

Santos's final images are, appropriately, of attenuation, nuance, and perfectibility—the air barely rippling some curtains, his mother fastidiously washing the still clean and unused plates, the images of ants airborne and beating suicidally against a light, dropping "their transparent / Wings on the water." This final image, in particular, might stand as metonym for the entire poem, representative as it is of frailty, obsession, and transformation—all qualities both of human limitation and potential, those very traits most evident in our private moments—the wings a delicate pattern, as if in evidence of purified being, on the insubstantial surface of water. It is tragic, exquisitely worked—the world aestheticized—and full of a rare evanescence of feeling attributable only to the act of the mind in contemplation, remembrance, and evocative return to the past it recaptures.

Yet it doesn't change the world so much as it changes, utterly, ultimately, only the poet and perhaps, ideally, a reader made an intimate by the experience. It changes him, or her, from a vacant nothing that produces the necessary somethings demanded by a hostile world into a privileged something, a consciousness that produces the nothing that is the poem, demanded by his, or her, most familiar self. Call it the poor man's Club Med vacation, if you like—it is, as Robert Frost said once, "the poem braving alien entanglements" and a blessed "momentary stay against confusion." Something we all desperately need, something, for lack of, our inner selves, in perpetual desperation, would die.

At times it seems lucky and unexpected, the past,
And who we were then, and what the mind brings
Back on an overcast day in late September,

The dense, evanescent clouds shifting overhead,
The wind fingering the branches in the live oaks,
The little chunks of our childhood selves

Floating to the surface after all these years
Like memories that we imagine we imagined. . . .
    Edward Hirsch

I'd like to close here by telling a story. I myself never thought much about the past, nor about how it made me different and it different from me, ultimately, until the summer I was ten and my parents sent me back to Hawai'i from L.A. after I'd been away three or four years. I went back to the places of my childhood first chance I got, ran off from my relatives assembled for a family picnic at our old hometown, and went deliriously for all my old haunts—the dirt pits of my marble games, the canefields that were my daytime hideaways blossoming with tassels, the downed and storm-ravaged tree trunk by the shore that served as castle and fort and private island. Miraculously, everything was still as I had left and remembered it, physically identical, but significantly different somehow, vacant of childhood feeling and delight, mysteriously more distant from me than they were even as memories. And I was stunned, flushed clean of feeling, suddenly detached from them all, until, losing my way back to the ball field and parade grounds where everyone was barbecuing and sipping Cokes and playing catch or flying kites on the picnic, I managed to get to an old military road running alongside the village from the main highway to the sea. I could hear the surf pounding away at the point in the distance, and I fell into a familiar step as I turned a narrow bend and came under the shade of a roadside stand of ironwood trees, hissing with the constant brush of the trades. Kahuku pines, we called them, familiarly, after the name of our own village, and I never did learn the proper name until this last year when I returned again, with my own family, to stay the summer. I kicked a little at the red drifts of needles piled by the shoulder, recalled games I'd played among the rough-bark trunks of the trees, and I was full of a new feeling, suffusing from the place and from memory, myself suddenly there and not there, part of the past and yet distant from it as Psyche was from Cupid. I remembered a day Army jeeps came through there, squeaking on their shocks, engines grunting like herded pigs, lost on maneuvers during an exercise, delighting us island kids with the impromptu display of military pomp and spectacle, funky and unintentional as it was. I felt soothed in my own skin finally, without the formidable restlessness that had been my torment up until then, and I could have stayed there for hours in that feeling, gigantic with my own emotions and memories, lifted out of myself and over the tops of those iron-wood trees, part of everything that surrounded me, except that, in order for the mood to persist, I had to keep walking, down the dirt road and to the park by the highway, and away, finally, from that mood entirely. I walked past the trees, alongside the rusted, corrugated iron fence of the village wrecking yard, by the swept, immaculate grounds of the Buddhist temple, and finally to the 76 station on the Kamehameha Highway. Before I crossed to the park and the picnic full of boisterous relatives lounging on their grass mats, I promised myself that I'd be back to get that feeling again. To do that, I think I had to become a poet, and writing poems, reading them, I try to take that walk all the time.

II

Ministry

Homage to Kīlauea

Living on the mainland and in cities these past few years, I have
grown confused about the earth. It had been my thought for a
long stretch of time during my middle thirties—those years I'd
lived in Volcano, Hawai'i, that village in the rain forest where I
was born—that one could learn to *belong* to a place, even a cho-
sen place, in a way that would feel like home, like an inheritance
of some spiritual and nonmaterial sort; that, in time, the mere
apprehension of a particular spot of earth would come to sing
out like a choir of its finest birds and extend you the gift of some
intimate warmth, almost like recognition, like kinship itself. It
was as if the natural features in a landscape were manifestations
of a sublime consciousness, that mountains and canyons, that
calderas and sea arches had something indwelling and harmoni-
ous with my soul's need for rest and acceptance. Not Maia's veil,
but the face of God.

Lately, though, I have felt otherwise, bereft, that these beliefs
are consolational fictions. That the earth, despite any of our af-
fections for it, is itself and spiritually inviolable, austere and re-
moved from any human homage or protestation. It is a lordly
and an inhumane magnificence. It is power and preciousness.
It is itself. *Dread.*

When this desolate feeling comes upon me, I know I have
been in cities too long. I know I need to make a small journey
and gaze upon the pure creation of earth. I go walking upon
volcanoes.

When my two boys were babies, to help them fall asleep in
the afternoons, I liked driving them out from the house we al-

81

ways rented in the village of Volcano, not three miles from the summit caldera of Kīlauea. We lived in Mauna Loa Estates, a pattern of subdivided lots cut out of the rain forest downslope of the volcano. Every day around three o'clock, I would drive my kids up the highway a mile or two through the park entrance, our little car plunging like a submarine past all the microclimates and botanical realities of tree ferns and runaway exotic gingers and bamboo orchids until we got to the swing in the road just before the turnout to Kīlauea observatory at Uwēkahuna Bluff. I'd pull over into a little gravel slot by the roadside and let all the air-conditioned tour buses and shining red rental cars and U.S. Geological Survey Cherokees and geologists' Broncos swoosh by while I took a long view over the dome of Kīlauea toward the veldt-like lower slopes of Mauna Loa, my boys already asleep in the backseat. It became part of a contemplative ritual for me—the afternoon drive with my children, then the pure gazing into a spectacular landscape. What I liked was the swoop of land, the way it rolled out from under my beach-sandaled feet, and the swimming air, freighted with clouds that seemed the land's vision rising over it. I always felt that I could have been the land's own dream then, and I liked thinking of myself that way, as offspring come to pay it the tribute of my own assembling thoughts, seeking the unearned coherence of apprehending beauty, little brainy cyclones that touched down in the lava channels or drained back into rivulets of wind. "Cloud and Man differ not," I'd joke to myself. "All is One under Heaven." And why not?

I thought in romantic rhythms; I thought: *What if we were to recast ourselves as descendants all gathered at the foot of our sponsoring mountains, drawn by a love like primitive magnetisms and convection currents calling all things back to their incarnate sources? What would be the point other than to step into the sulfuric cleansing of volcanic clouds? Our dithyrambs of dream-mountains not quite earth's equal but more vague than that—like clouds around Mauna Loa, drifting continents of vapor and dust riding the gyring wind-gusts over Halemaʻumaʻu and Iki, mantlings of evanescence on the tropical shoulders of an angel? Aren't we the earth become known to itself, I thought, Homo sapiens celebrants of a sublime not completely dreadful, but companionable too, its presence like two sleeping children, innocent dragons fogging the car's rear window with a visible breath?*

A few years ago, a friend from the Mainland, a poet and literary critic, flew to visit me in my remote seclusion from the literary world. My friend is immersed in the fray of the *New York Times Book Review, Poetry,* and the *New Yorker,* and I value his insights and opinions. In the few days of his stay, I took him to lookouts and photo opportunities around the volcano while we schmoozed on about editors and poetry readings, about book contracts and creative writing programs, about museum shows and the NBA playoffs.

We circumnavigated the caldera counterclockwise along the road named Crater Rim Drive. I spouted on about the cloud-magnet that Mauna Loa was, how it gathered its weather every day, wearing a skirt of clouds at about the 6,500-foot level by the time three o'clock rolled around. I stopped at various lookout points: a little roadside rise near the volcano observatory inside the National Park; a pullout overlooking the hogback-shaped fumaroles of what was once a "curtain of fire" eruption along Kīlauea's northern caldera floor; a turnout next to Keanakakoi, a smallish pit crater where we could see the ragged earth drop 600 feet to an almost smooth black lava floor; the viewpoint over Iki where I'd once seen schoolchildren on a field trip and heard them singing as they crossed the caldera; the still, quiet arena at the rain forest near there where the tree line grew a little higher and the tree ferns and false staghorns thickened over patchy hot spots still heating through the undergrowth.

After a couple of days of this, I realized I was turning botanical and geologic wonders into patter, spiel, and personal history, giving my friend a kind of live slideshow presentation of the volcano. As an antidote, I decided we should hike across the short, flat trail from a turnout along the Chain of Craters Road toward a dormant lava cone, centuries old, named Puʻu Huluhulu. I wanted to show him the lava trees along the way. They were the remains of a forest burned down by one of the recent flows during the seventies. Lava trees form in the aftermath of the movement of a large flow of *pāhoehoe,* that viscous lava, through a stand of *ʻōhiʻa* or *hāpuʻu,* the native myrtle and gigantic tree fern of Hawaiʻi. *Pāhoehoe* streams through the grove of trees, incinerating bark and branches, but flowing around the fatter trunks, cooling down, forming lava casts around the burning trees as the flow ebbs away.

A little path ran *makai* (seaward) of the remnant grove we walked through. Huge geoducks and horse penises of black spinnakered glass stood out from the flow. These were forbidding snags formed around tree ferns and *ʻōhiʻa*—spires of *pāhoehoe* left behind while the flow had driven on. Encased in lava, the trunk wood incinerated and burned, leaving centers filled with charcoal and ash, slowly hollowing out in every breath of fresh wind. When everything cooled and became solid, what was left was a Grove of Suicides—Dante's fiery souls trapped in the remains of trees that bled black rock at their joints and seams, that shattered and flaked when you touched them, that, from a distant view, made a plain of charred stubble under dark, drenching skies. I wrapped an arm around one and, though I felt life and not death there, the rock tree more a shriveled and torn umbilical than the condemned form of one of Dante's sinners, I sensed how another could imagine an ending coming to the earth and our time on it, a forest of green sacrificed to this black of a new beginning, to me a froth of redemption.

My friend snapped photos for a while, and I sensed the visit was becoming mechanical. He was at a loss out there on the black expanse of lava. It was the moment of turning as with any freighted experience or relationship. A line of activity exhausts itself and must change. The fires of that wild ecstasy for the world and poetry we had shared in our youth had banked some, and we were moving, if only slightly, away from each other.

He gestured to a bomb of rock near me. His face had brightened and the cloud of emotions or boredom had cleared. He picked up the fractured white limb of an *ʻōhiʻa* and swung it like a baseball bat. He wanted a pitch, a game. I was perplexed, but I picked up a piece of rock and lobbed it like a softball, low and away. Ready for it, he took a swing and missed, laughing.

I thought of our friendship, how it was built on the way we each cherished the particular histories of the other's family, how both of us, during our college years and years of apprenticeship in the art, had taught ourselves ways to love the world through reading its many poets—Neruda of Chile, Li Po and Tu Fu of China, Whitman of Manhattan and Brooklyn and New Jersey, Yeats of Ireland. Yet I was moving away from books now and into something else I thought might eventually mean more—I felt I was moving toward the land. Perhaps even *my* land. It felt odd to me to be playing this boyhood game out on the plain of lava trees. But I went along, tossing the different pieces of lava I could find, trying to recapture a feeling for each other. It all felt so dissonant to me, though I tried to lighten my heart to match his frivolity, getting into the sport and mock competition of it all.

"That's a double," he'd say, shattering a slab of frothy rock and sending its largest fragment over my head and fifteen yards over the slick surface of the hardened flow.

"That's a pop-up," I'd say, or, "Strike three, side retired." White spider chrysanthemums of clouds opened against the blue azimuth of sky overhead. The concussive *whup-whup* of a helicopter went off far away.

The first time I'd visited Volcano, I was filled with the immensities of realization and resolve. It was like an eclipse—the wolf of the moon devouring the sun. Yet it could not captivate my friend, and all my blather about it seemed only to have gotten in the way. He was not as susceptible to this volcanic beauty. I knew that in his poetry he took inspiration from paintings and modern music, from life in American cities of the East and Midwest, and from poets of the European past. His concern was the desolation in human spirit after the fall of civilization, yet again, even after the brilliant optimism of our America. We were brothers escaping the old literary myths, living in passion and different histories, poets of sentiment improvising a way to speak and to act while living on the earth.

At play on that lava field, we began talking about what fuels creative acts, how we'd each found our own ways to make poems. I bent down and took a pinch of brown silica, called Pele's hair, between my fingers. There was amber and viridian and bronze all apparent in the fine fibers of rock. I tossed them away and told him that the wish to make poetry had begun as an ineffable *feeling* for me, one I didn't necessarily have words for. I tried to take it and let it lap up inside of me, a hollow chamber of being, until it filled the imagination the way lava plumes upward from its reservoir in inner earth, spouting to the surface in gouts of red display. I said I had to stay quiet, until I could see clear through a feeling that has made itself. I took inspiration from that feeling and tried to let words come from that in whatever shape they formed themselves—blossoms or fire-fountains.

"And the problem of making?" he said, excited now. "Didn't you try to shape the poem somehow? Isn't form mostly a way to build ceremony into the act of making words?"

"Form is helpful," I said, "but do we ever start with that? I always need that voice or an image that beguiles the mind, and then I wait for a *mood* to grow around that voice or that image. I try to listen to that voice, then *speak* in that voice, and I try not to direct it too much. I *listen* and I try to live in feeling."

"But how do you do that?" my friend asked. His face had wrapped itself into a thoughtful scowl. "Doesn't form and what traditions have taught us give us the tools to *stay* in the feeling, even perfect it? Can't form be a meditative tool? A way to catch the heat of a falling star?"

I saw that the far horizon had become whitened with fog behind his shoulders, that gray seas of lava spread just below the sky, that the radiance of black mounds and furled rock surrounded us.

"I try not to be too busy," I said. "Being involved with the world hurts the feeling."

Standing among the lava trees near Puʻu Huluhulu, I felt a little guilty—that I was disloyal to the land somehow. I worried that we were playing out the rules of a nineteenth-century summer game and not finding a way to respond with fitting ceremony to the stark landscape before us. My friend tossed the lava rocks toward me, and I swung the burnt limb of a tree. My ghosts and sponsoring gods were not his.

Yet I pointed to the buff-colored lava hill nearby.

"See that old cinder cone?" I said. "Doesn't it give you a feeling that's not in words?"

He turned and scanned the black sea of *pāhoehoe* around us. Lava trees stippled the plain in the distance. The sky shaped itself into an azure bowl of pure peace.

"Consciousness is the lotus dropped in a bowl," I said.

I sensed wraiths curling in the fumaroles and in the mists rising from the line of lava trees farther toward the live vent of Kīlauea. A lavish, druglike melancholy crept into my blood. Out of my body, from the gigantic lens of the sky, I could gaze down and see us standing on the little plain of black jars by the lava hill of Puʻu Huluhulu.

My friend indulged me and took in that black expanse of looking too. He was gazing off into the middle distance down the big volcanic rift in the earth. Beyond the fog line, from hill to crater and spatter cone to caldera, there was a dancer spinning out from her wrap of living rock, twirling seaward in red veils.

"Maybe ceremony could be the earth itself," he said, his face still away from me. "And words our mortal acts upon it—little shards of glory."

He turned and wheeled back to me then, suddenly, twirling his body and catching me off guard. An ink-dark piece of lava zinged past my chest. I heard it cut the air.

"Strike two!" he shouted, laughing again. My elder, gifted with a lulling sympathy and tricks of beguilement.

Before I could complain, he twirled once more and pitched me a soft, easy toss. I took a breath, then made a slow swing that connected. The splinter of lava, black as asphalt, skipped along the silver shine on the old flow's surface. We called it on that.

When we walked away, back toward the car before sunset, the black trees at our backs stood like sentinels of the afterlife, dread outfielders spaced over an earth before there was grass.

I've been looking at Kīlauea, the active volcano on the island of Hawaiʻi, and its various eruptive features for a few years now, and every time I do it, I really never know what it is I'll be looking at, looking for, remembering, or comparing it to. It's kind of like daydreaming, gazing at the birth-stem of all things.

This looking is a rapturous privacy and it follows whatever are the specifics of the earthly phenomenon that is before me—a fissure line of rupture in the earth fuming with sulfurous air; a glistening beach of newborn black sand; a conical driblet spire crowning a fresh flow that, out of its blowhole, spouts an incandescent emission like red sperm over the new land; solidified eddies of *pāhoehoe* swirled like fans of pandanus leaves inundating Highway 130 near Kaimū; or a frozen cascade of lava sluiced over a low dun-colored bluff that foregrounds a deep-focus panorama over the sublime shades of gray and black plain of Ka'ū Desert, the mother's breast of my universe.

When I first came upon hot spots and volcanoes—whether it was the soft buff-colored lava domes of Mammoth Lakes in the eastern Sierra Nevada, the boiling earthy soups of foamy hot springs in Yellowstone Park, or the long, whale-like profile of Hawai'i's Mauna Loa—I became aware that I was before a deep mystery that shocked and yet seemed to work subtly too, driving through the green thigh of imagination, reminding me, as my thoughts formed themselves into faintly tidal rhythms of realization and befuddlement, of what was quintessential mystery—questions of poetry and creation. My mind and soul turned in a dance, squiring each other, revolving like twin stars in a galaxy of lavas flowing in a slow, mortal spiral down the bole of a frightened tree standing in its path, its crown a fan of gray coral, creating a form out of fire and extinguishment, a frothy, snakelike cone of astral matter descending the blazing trunk of an *'ōhi'a* tree burning to ash and char.

I heard a song inside of me. I had a little vision of schoolchildren crossing not a village green in London or gamboling through a countryside dotted with barns and farm ponds, but over an Alaskan plain of smokes, over a dire lake of black lavas transformed into the congenial earth they could walk upon. There simply was everything to think about, and my mind, in those moments, seemed suddenly capable of thinking them all, holding them in one breath's time, the 10,000 things of creation's entirety caught in the spirit's dance of my apprehending. A body made electric by them. It was an ocean of thoughts broader than the dark and immense plain of lavas I crossed one moonlit night driving through northern Idaho. If I know immensity, it is that piece of earth that taught it to me. *Craters of the Moon* means a dread expansiveness; means *I will be hours with one thought, one sensation*; means a reckoning of language to pure creation. All of learning, faith, and human effort can be subsumed in that momentary awareness.

Living near Kīlauea, the looking gives me details that, in the mind, pile against each other like clouds against Mauna Loa, subductions and effervescences shoring like seas against a continent. Recollecting takes meditation, another daydream, and then something like a vision comes:

If I drove up from the rain forest and through the park, plunging past all the microclimates of rain-beaded ginger lilies and the scorched forest of ʻōhiʻa and false staghorn ferns dying in the suffocating sulfuric fogs of Steaming Bluffs, crossing the sinkbowl of a tiny caldera matted with ferns and sedges, I'd get to a mound of land near Uwēkahuna where I can look out over the inflatable summit dome of Kīlauea rising over a long slot of pulverized lavas, buff and brown in sunny weather. If I stopped and pulled over, if I walked out onto the roll of the land giving way to shallow faults and gullies, an inner sea of unstable rock frequented with seismic swarms and churning with a hundred rises as if the gathering pods of khaki-backed migrating whales were spuming their way from there toward Mauna Loa, I would see a long black groove that would be Volcano Highway twisting through the gully that is the seam of earthen creation where the land, churning with perceptible movement, becomes Mauna Loa, an earthform concerto building slowly through basaltic gradients of blue and gray into the summit caldera obscured by clouds, dwarfed by the inverted bowl of the afternoon sky's pale porcelain blue. I would lean against an onrush of wind scudding over the plain of lavas, sent by the flattening heel of a cloud bank, stratocumulus, insubstantial wraith skydiving in the space between heaven and Kīlauea, between one volcano and another.

And if I reached beside me, scrubby boughs of ʻōhelo bushes would be cowlicking like the thick fur between the shoulders of a wolf or bear, ruffled alert by wind of the scent of humans walking close by. Shining berries, some a deep red, others more pale, some of them spotted with blemishes, would bounce with a sugary weight against my hand as I bent to pluck them.

The land and its atmosphere will have gathered themselves into whatever act the clouds and I might bring about: a tribute of afternoon rain, garlands of purple trailing like a fringed skirt under the moving clouds, a handful of tiny fruit, unstrung, juicy pearls tossed from my hand into the scuffed canyonlands of eroded lavas reaching out to me from a sullen sleep.

I will have roused this rock into the space of my own living. It is music. It is the sweet scent of rain spuming puffed quarter notes of dust on the land.

And if I turned to leave, back toward my car parked by the side of the road, I would be through with looking, my body shuffled against the wind like a tree, red-brilliant, full of passionate blossoms too heavy for its boughs, the long mountain at my back, pure upwelling of Kīlauea in my soul, the dancer and the dance, kin to earth again.

For Edward Hirsch

A Man on a Child's Swing

Contemporary Japanese Poetry

Let me start with an image from Japanese cinema—it is of a man singing, the old bureaucrat played by Takashi Shimura in Akira Kurosawa's *Ikiru*, a drama of contemporary life. The man's name is Watanabe, and he sings something desperate, poignant, and off-key as he sits in a child's swing in a small park somewhere in the gray ruin of postwar Tokyo. We know from the film's narrative that Watanabe has been diagnosed with terminal cancer and that none of his coworkers or family is able to give a damn. He's spent a few nights prowling Tokyo's nightlife for its dizzying myriad of cheap distractions—until he meets a sweet bar girl who has a child in whom he takes an interest. Their relationship is chaste but then begins to convulse. Empowered by fear and a newly aroused compassion, Watanabe comes up with a plan to influence his moribund municipal office to build a playground. He struggles to build human connections, redeem a life without relationships, without meaning. Finally, through a twist, he succeeds, and, in a scene late in the movie, we find him, still dressed in his long coat and business clothes, seated happily on a child's swing during a snowfall. Kurosawa's 35 mm black-and-white film captures the flurry as amulets of insight falling on the somewhat outsize hat and mortal shoulders of "salary man" suddenly made joyous. Watanabe will have his park! He has transformed his own dedicated, incremental misery into a site for the temporal amusement of children.

This is the story of modern Japanese poetry too. It rises from the spiritual, dehumanizing torpor of lives confused and ruined through the long century of Japan's Westernization, industrialization, and militarization since Commodore Matthew Perry's black ships forced the opening of Yokohama Bay to foreign trade in 1866. Nearly a century later, by the time of Kurosawa's film, so much social change and cultural displacement, so much true upheaval had called all that had been traditional into question. It was thus with traditional Japanese poetry as well. The old forms of *tanka* and *haiku* spoke for other times, in languages that were fairly restrictive, not only in terms of diction and grammar, but even in vocabulary. A traditional *tanka* or *haiku* poet could not mention all the new things—a steam locomotive, an iron bridge, foreign sailors on liberty gathering at Tokyo Station, an atom bomb. The old literary practices, for all their fabled charm, were almost exclusively bucolic and came couched in a language all too literary—a language that had quickly become a "foreign" one.

The new poets initially responded by revamping traditional forms like the *haiku* and the *tanka*, incorporating not only new vocabularies but the new, angst-ridden moods, and the more libertarian view of personal identities and appropriate poetic subjects. Shiki Masaoka (1867–1902) wrote *haiku* about drying socks as well as wisteria blossoms. Akiko Yosano (1878–1942) wrote vivid *tanka* about her own erotic life, mentioning breasts and thighs and the sated tenderness after lovemaking. And Takuboku Ishikawa (1886–1912) brought into the stately *tanka* the sounds of tubercular breathing and footfalls of wandering drunks. The overall difference was an embracing of spleen, eroticism, and the humbler items of modern life in exchange for the sweet chorus of pond frogs and images of a silvery snow falling on the thatched rooflines of a far-off village glimpsed at sunset.

Yet the largest revolution was the complete abandonment of traditional forms altogether and the invention of a Japanese free verse reflective of some tradition but responsive to contemporary life. Called *jiyuritsushi*, or literally "free-style poetry," this new form had, to my mind, three important early practitioners, each with their own stylistically recognizable way of handling the problem of creating a vernacular poetry out of the modern Japanese language—two secular intellectuals, Sakutaro Hagiwara and Junzaburo Nishiwaki, and a supremely religious one, Kenji Miyazawa.

When Sakutaro Hagiwara (1886–1942) published *Howling at*

the Moon in 1917, the new poetry finally had its first, full-fledged champion. Modern spoken Japanese, full of Western neologisms and the unromanticized cares of harried, newly urbanized lives, at last arrived as a poetic language in Hagiwara. The work is entirely in the free style, almost exclusively in the modern language, yet there are shades of archaism, unexpected twists of syntax, and a deep melancholy about modern life. One of my favorite poems of his was written after he separated from his wife and retreated to his parents' village, bringing his two young daughters on the long train trip from Tokyo to the provinces. Other poems take howling dogs and the corpse of a cat as fitting subjects for poetry, like John Donne's flea and Alan Dugan's mouse caught in a trap, which then occasion metaphysical flight and existential reflection.

That Junzaburo Nishiwaki (1894–1982) published his first volume of poetry, *Spectrum,* in English and not Japanese tells us how ambitious, cosmopolitan, and erudite a poet he was. Nishiwaki was also an editor, a professor of English literature, and a noted theorist on poetics. He went on to publish (in Japanese) about twenty volumes of poetry, several works of translation (Chaucer, Shakespeare, Eliot, and so on), a history of modern English literature, and yet another book of poems in English. Ezra Pound said in 1956, after reading Nishiwaki's English poem "January in Kyoto," that "Junzaburo has a more vital english than any I have seen for some time." In translation, his work has that sense of being a kind of "freed verse" close to Eliot's in "Preludes." His sentences scroll out, somewhat Latinate, with a dazzling rhetorical finish, references to literature and foreign travel, and precise botanical descriptions. Yet it is a fulsome poetry, not unlike Pablo Neruda's of the *Residencias* period, exhilarated with human potential, a surrealist's sense of drama, and a deep, gigantic loneliness.

In Japan today Kenji Miyazawa (1896–1933) is perhaps the most commonly read of the three I've cited, but he was far from well known during his own lifetime. The son of a pawnbroker in Iwate, then a fairly remote prefecture in northern Japan, Miyazawa was formally educated in Buddhism and agriculture. He taught literature, English, and science at various schools during his early professional life, but later turned mainly to farming and a life as a kind of volunteer field agent/adviser to the peasants in the district where he was born. He published *Spring and the Ashura* in 1924 with his own money. He continued writing what he called "image sketches" in various notebooks until 1933, when he succumbed to an illness made fatal by his refusal to leave his work in the fields. Three unpublished volumes of poetry were found among his papers, each with the same title as his first book. The modern vernacular of his verse, full of agrarian life and a deep concern for farmers among whom he worked, reflects both his personal humility and a devout Buddhist philosophy. Although highly accessible, a provocative Buddhist and scientific vocabulary adds weight and majesty to this sublimely humane life's work.

After these three, Japanese poetry had accomplished its vernacular style, but had yet to respond to the emotionally bleak and economically arduous period following World War II. The militarism and state-sponsored industrial optimism that made up so much of the zeitgeist of prewar Japan had been discredited and abandoned, but not yet replaced. There was a "lost" period, filled by the cultural work of novelists and filmmakers who concentrated on the efforts of Japanese society, through its individuals, to reconstruct itself. Films by Yasujiro Ozu portrayed the new instabilities confronting the Japanese family. Kurosawa made other movies (like *Ikiru*) that placed a lost individual at the center. Novels by Michio Takeyama (*Harp of Burma*), Masuji Ibuse (*Black Rain*), and Shohei Ooka (*Fires on the Plain*)—all subsequently made into films—took close, hard looks at the material and spiritual costs of war. Eventually a kind of "consensus of pain" had developed, centering around the works of novelists like Osamu Dazai (*The Setting Sun*), champion of the narrative of suicide.

This was the situation that confronted the new, postwar generation of modern Japanese poets. They did not have to invent a vernacular style but to counteract the circumstances of a bleak, fragmenting society and an exploded traditional culture. Like the Americans of the Beat Generation, their response was a poetry of vigor and newborn innocence that celebrated mundanities as if they were miracles, that raised the rude and humble to the level of provisional splendor. I have chosen to focus, among the many talented and prolific poets of this group, on Shuntaro Tanikawa.

Tanikawa was born in an intellectual family in Tokyo in 1931, the son of a philosopher and a pianist. He began publishing in magazines when he was twenty. In 1952, by the time he was twenty-two, he published his first collection, *The Loneliness of Twenty Million Light Years*. Encouraged by a group of poets around the magazine *Kai* ("Oar"), he went on to write libretti, radio plays, scripts for television and films, and several more volumes of poetry. He is perhaps the best-known poet of the postwar generation.

Overall Tanikawa concerns himself with strongly humanitarian themes expressed in rhythmic, highly accessible common language. "Nero," an early poem, takes up the topic of the death of his pet dog and lifts this humble consideration toward a real amplitude of thought and feeling. Yet humor and surprise are important features throughout his work, and his poems have a kind of "lightness" akin to that of contemporary tragicomic writers like the Czech novelist Milan Kundera, the Polish poet Zbigniew Herbert, and the American poet Charles Simic. Tanikawa mocks exaggerated pathos, sneezes at literary tragedies, and reviles familiar sanctities.

"After the defeat," he writes, speaking of the postwar period, "all the values that the Japanese had believed in were completely destroyed. It was a period of vacuum for us and nobody knew what to believe." What Tanikawa accomplished, along with others of his generation, is a poetry that urges the disconsolate, postwar sensibility to begin again through its affinities for the first, simplest things—a land, animals, a partner and children under a blue sky, and a place for children to play. His work, like that of any singer's caught out in the rain, like that of *Ikiru's* once-dour Watanabe exalted by a self-born vision into joy, has been no less a task than the reconstruction of a humane cosmos.

Review of *Turning Japanese*
Memoirs of a Sansei *by David Mura*

"I am a *Sansei*, a third-generation Japanese American. In 1984, through luck and through some skills as a poet, I traveled to Japan. My reasons for going were not very clear."

These spare sentences declare the problems and cruxes of an extraordinarily wise and moving book, *Turning Japanese: Memoirs of a Sansei* by Minnesota poet David Mura. The work describes, in an understated but powerful lyrical prose reminiscent of novelist Richard Ford's, Mura's yearlong sojourn in Japan, the country of his ancestry. From the start, it takes up themes of personal and racial identities and the plot of questing for them, anxieties about descent from East Asian culture and immigration history and the author's modest yet powerful consciousness that he is both a poet and a member of an American minority. And, through all of its roughly 350 pages, every passage is imbued with the tone and undercurrent of emotion of someone who has been a voyeuristic witness to his own transformation. It is as if the hermaphroditic and urbane offspring of the uncouth woodcutter and raped courtesan in *Rashōmon* has turned up to give us testimony to its origin in a dark wood. For *Turning Japanese* has the excitement of prurience to it, possessing a gentle eroticism, as Mura's personal, nearly obsessively narcissistic revelations plash softly against a surreal, eclectic backdrop of the jumbled, ravished world of postmodern Japan.

Mura recreates the freewheeling maelstrom of his Japanese year (Tokyo sushi bars, the bullet train to Kyoto, radical-student demonstrations, Noh chant and Butoh dance, coffeehouse bull sessions with other foreigners and the Japanese, brushes with illicit sex) in a narrative screen painting of interconnected yet lyrically discrete scenes and characterizations. As an amateur journalist self-assigned to the task of reportage, Mura is perfectly accurate in his descriptions, a Sansei Daniel Defoe on a walk through the entire islands of greater Japan. He revels in the sensuous world of the Japanese, responding with awe and quiescence in the face of traditional beauty, with amusement and affection when confronted with amalgams of the contemporary. This is Mura on something recognizably classical:

> The play was *Dōjōji*, a special Noh performance. On the bare floor, the masked dancer robed in green and gold glided in circles, never lifting his feet between steps, only his toes rising at the end of each stride, like a sigh. . . . His mask was gold, the twisted features of a demon. Behind him the great cedar painted on the back of the Noh stage spread its stillness. The dancer turned, pounded out calls: the *taiko* drummer's short and abrupt, the *otsuzumi* drummer's high and long, almost a yodel. The flute flew up and down like a leaf in a whirlwind. Seated to the side of the stage on their knees, like a row of candles, the chorus droned, chanted.

And this, Mura on the nearly absurd charm of the postmodern:

> Along the main street near the station, the shops spilled out their goods. Racks of shoes, pottery, towels, magazines; bins of oranges, apples, bananas, signs with kanji, photographs of sushi. A plastic, life-size Colonel Sanders, like a bizarre, transformed Buddha. . . . An old woman in a kimono paused to look at a window. The rubbery smell of udon wafted from a doorway.

Though a thoughtful, confessional mode dominates the book and allows him an honest, postmodern bewilderment, there are numerous passages fraught with romantic expectation. Poised on a mountaintop, he muses:

> Something settled inside me. I had come on a journey. . . . My writing, that was the center of my life. Did there need to be something more . . . ? I spent a long while at the top of that mountain, wandering through the pines and cedars, the trunks that rose forty, fifty, sixty feet over my head. In the thick

97

dark, amid the smell of the needles, I felt a sense of uncanniness, of whatever was Japanese inside me, suddenly palpable and present in the wind that flowed around my body. . . . It was so familiar, so familial, that peace.

The persona he develops—that of the poetic hero weighing and evaluating each item of the freshly encountered culture, every evocation of the past—could be cloying were Mura's writing not so brave, modest, and appealing. Worshipping at the ancient Shinto shrines of Ise, he claps twice and thanks his parents, his grandparents, and calls on the ancestral land for his own mental peace. And there is no nostalgia, no self-conscious clichés of ethnic pride, but only resolve and a pious filiality. With throngs of Japanese, he exits a Tokyo train and files into Kyoto Station, sensing his own face and figure are lost in the swirl of racial likenesses surrounding him. Mura feels safe, anonymous, accepted. The attaché sent to meet him from the American Center, where he is to give a poetry reading, expects someone in casual denims—a scruffy poet and not the fashion-conscious, smart-set Edoite Mura—and loses him in the crowd, forcing the Sansei poet to make his own way through the strange city.

Through each hilarious or poignant scene, Mura interweaves his supply-written meditations, providing commentary on the exotic experiences, but not in the programmatic manner of the bored, Victorian traveler nor with the acid cynicism of the more contemporary, postcolonial laureate. By contrast to these imperious chroniclers of travel, Mura is the vulnerable American, often an ingénue without design but simply thirsty for knowledge and an introduction into the hidden meanings of things, a kind of forgiving voyeur spying into the soul of his own life. He is a poet, seeking a simple nature yet possessed of baroque qualities of imagination and vast learning.

The heady drafts of this book are indeed his tale-spinnings and meditations, and there is genius in the divagations of his thoughts as they drift toward contemplations of the past, to ramblings on literary histories, both Japanese and Western, to questions of personal identity and his relationship to white America. When Mura recalls his upbringing in Chicago—the successive moves from lower-class to working-class to middle-class urban neighborhoods, until finally his stoical Nisei businessman father moves them to the upper-middle-class suburbs—he ends by considering the resolute silence of the Nisei, determined to leave the failed and shameful history of wartime relocation camps behind them. There is a scene in which his father, in a rage at his rebelliousness and the state of the country during the sixties, forces Mura to submit to a shearing of his long hair the day before he is to leave for college.

The moment is, of course, dramatic and an obvious symbol of their generational conflict, yet Mura lifts the scene above this banal level by joining it to another one that is terrifying, pathetic, and illuminating. It is an afternoon years later, during his twenties, and he and his white girlfriend are in the bathroom of their tiny apartment "on the Native American side of town." Bright and determined, she will later become his wife, a medical doctor, and his main companion and interlocutor throughout the sojourn and the rest of his life. Mura is applying a foamy dye to her brown hair in order to streak it blonde and give it a sexual, truck-stop cheapness she will hate and he will want more of. Describing her submissiveness under the lavish hiss of the absurd aerosol spray, a sheet spread over her body, he retrieves the image of his Nisei father bending to rape the long hair of David the teenager and superimposes it over the momentarily pliant figure of this powerful woman, who is descended from Mayflower Wasps and Hungarian Jews. When Mura writes, "It is a sign that she loves me," he cauterizes both scenes in the powerful irony of self-recognition and complicity. He invokes race and sex in the juxtaposition, accomplishes a savvy critique of power, challenges all claims of unearned love in ancestry and marriage, and telescopes the complex of racial tensions in his life into these doubled submissions.

This raising of the mundane to profundity is characteristic of Mura's deft and temporally fluid imagination. His consciously lapidary method with the narrative gives the entire project the authority of enlightenment and civilization that is the essential quality of the grandest literary confessions. Something quite savage is, for the moment, in these very scenes of writing, made nearly gentle.

His first book, *After We Lost Our Way* (Dutton, 1989), was a strong collection of eclectic narratives and lyrics that won a place in the prestigious National Poetry Series. *Turning Japanese* is his second book, and, though subtitled as a memoir, it is as properly a *confessio* as a reminiscence. Mura's work compares to a whole catalogue of titles in the genre. Like Petrarch, he writes with grace and simplicity of style; like Augustine's, his imagination is capable of sustained rococo meditation; like Sei Shonagon, he is possessed of a finely tuned wit. Yet, it is his confrontation of painful, personal, and racial conflicts that makes this work unique and inspires his most compelling writing. One thinks of Richard Rodriguez's recent memoir as a possible analogue— like Rodriguez, Mura writes beautifully and confronts the familial and racial past with courage—but, as I was reading through it, the book seemed most like Rian Malan's *My Traitor's Heart*, the story of a self-exiled and outlawed Afrikaner's conscientiously deliberated return to his severely troubled homeland. Like the South African's, Mura's book is a saga from a postexistentialist perspective that might serve as a contemporary guide to perplexed world travelers and displaced persons who have not so much lost secure identities and homelands as the abiding need—perhaps classical and outmoded—to maintain them. Mura is something new—a clumsy cosmopolitan, a dandy, a worried innocent and befuddled intellectual traveler and a lover of contradictions—one who occupies the margins and revels in his own belatedness and cultural *différence*.

Forever odd and uncomfortable without the Ur-text of an absolute culture that he can identify with and that will guide social actions and define his psychic patterns, he is the perpetual outsider—the Asian among yuppie Minnesota Protestants, the oafish American among Japanese, the poet among *sarariman*. Once, back in high school in a Chicago suburb near Skokie, a Jewish teammate taunts him during basketball practice about his race, his geekiness, and his adolescent eczema. Mura rages inside, maintaining the unendurable silence, yet reacts gracefully, passing the Jew the ball on the drive for an assist. So it is with Mura's book. He does not hate, either himself or the tripartite worlds of Japan, America, and Japanese America. Nor is he revolted or defeated by their differences. He makes out of them and for himself, through his immensely gifted meditative and appreciative writing, a sublime and gentle place as poetic legislator in each of these worlds. His *Turning Japanese* is an extraordinary contribution and a necessary book for our richly complicated time.

Homage to Lost Worlds
Where I Write, Why I Write There

I constantly find myself having to *counteract* what pop and post-modern culture provide me as scenic and narrative identities, backdrops for the play of consciousness, yet they have the appeal of mass (mis)recognition, visual referents others can attach to a story I'm telling, in prose or poetry, about Hawai'i, my childhood place. And I am likewise constantly inspired by the great works of literature not to give in, to find inspiration in the humble regions of my own memory, in a homebound ethicality, in the sere commonplaces of mild existence. I have found *Walden* as our American version of the great Japanese eremitic *zuihitsu* (poetic essay) tradition practiced by Kamo-no-Chōmei, Yoshida Kenkō, and Matsuo Bashō. And I know that I write from lost places, neighborhoods I have been taken away from I feel a need to return to.

I want to look at geo-cultural locations and dislocations, collisions of, not geologic plates or continents, but of circumstances wherein consciousness shifts when it travels and meets and feels affection for or even rejects different landscapes, cityscapes, and cultural matrixes associated with radical origin or, alternatively, radical change. If there is a "geography of the self'," that theory from Romanticism that says that the forms of one's own gravitate to items of the natural world, humanizing the landscape as a personal history as Wordsworth did the Wye Valley as a child, as Thoreau did with Walden Pond, then what happens when the landscape changes or is degraded or when a person migrates or a people are removed from homelands? What happens when the foreigner becomes American? When there is diaspora? What do we do when the self is estranged from lands?

I write from Kahuku, the plantation village on Oʻahu in Hawaiʻi where I grew up as a child, remembering its Buddhist temple, tofu makers, rows of shotguns, and sandy village square, remembering the fields of sugar cane, the tractors and trailers hauling burned and cut cane down the Kamehameha Highway to the smoking mill at the center of everything. I write from the rocky beaches and sandy promontories where the separate graveyards were for Filipino, Chinese, and Japanese workers. I write from the blossoming plumeria trees, from the ironwoods by the beaches, and my memory of street vendors' calls and my grandfather singing in Hawaiian and Japanese as he washed dishes for his roadside café. I write from this world I left at the age of six, returned to when I was ten, that was lost to everyone as the capitalized world of Hawaiʻi itself turned from sugar to tourism.

I write from the small tract home my parents bought for us in Gardena, near Los Angeles, its symmetrical grid of suburban streets, its corner gas stations and liquor stores, the barbed wire around my high school, the razor wire around wrecking yards and auto shops, the tiny Japanese *okazuya* and gaudy poker parlors, the rat-nests of palm trees, and the long, cooling, fog-banked, and wind-tunneled seaward-bound road at the center of town. I write from my memories of all of us in high school—black kids bused in from Compton, Chicanos from "The Tracks" near Gardena Boulevard, and us Buddhaheads from all over town, worried about dress and the latest dances, worried about cool and avoiding addiction to glue and Robitussin even as we hoped we were college-bound. I write about the summer evening Festival for the Dead at Gardena Hongwanji and the intimate spaces of dinnertime cooking my mother and grandmother made, my father watching football and boxing on the TV, exhausted after work and stymied by his social isolation. I write from people who work and want better for themselves and their children.

And I write from what was an intellectual native ground— my years away at Pomona College, where I studied literature, languages, and philosophy and was allowed to develop my deep love for learning and reflection. I found "the better nature" of literary practices there, sponsored in my soul a feel for the finish of language, the finer tone of contemplative emotions. What was better than reading Chaucer in the mornings, hearing a lecture on jazz operas and *Moby-Dick* by the fiery and entertaining Stanley Crouch, browsing through the home library of the poet Bert Meyers and hearing him hold forth on the Spanish Civil War and the poetry of Miguel Hernández? What was better than reading Chinese poetry late at night, having a cup of Burgundy, and practicing ideograms until I fell asleep over the smearing ink on the soft, absorbent pages of my copybook? *A line from Yeats runs through my head as I walk across the yellowing grass of a soccer field. It's a late spring twilight, the moon ascends over a snow-streaked Mt. Baldy in the distance, and I feel a studious complacency aroused into passion. . . .*

Volcano, the little village where I was born on the island of Hawai'i, is, finally, the first lost neighborhood of my soul. I did not grow up there in that preternatural rain forest and sublime volcanic landscape, but I moved back there many times these last few years, writing from the ache of my love for that place. It exceeds all the praise of lyric description I can muster. *Poet, take nothing from this world but awe and a longing to return to the magnificent beginnings of first things.*

Working for the DWP

Every summer between school years while I was in college, I worked as a seasonal meter reader for the Department of Water and Power of the City of Los Angeles. This meant that I spelled regular workers over the summer months so that they could take their vacations, about two weeks long each. As there was an entire pool of meter readers, this meant I worked throughout the summer months.

My job was to walk a given route each day, taking me through just about every neighborhood in L.A., from the Van Owen Reservoir in the San Fernando Valley to the loading docks and canneries on Terminal Island in San Pedro, and make readings of the electric and water meters. I walked the Chicano neighborhoods in the hills around Dodger Stadium and read water meters buried in the dirt. I strode briskly through neighborhoods in Watts where I saw children "walking" pet cockroaches on a makeshift leash of thread or string. I've had a shotgun trained on me through a peephole, a policeman sweep his sidearm past me tracking a fleeing thief, and Dobermans and German Shepherds and Rotweilers pursuing me, foaming at the mouth. I read meters throughout the Hollywood Hills and saw a beautiful rock star stark naked walking her pet Afghan hounds around her spacious backyard. I read George Harrison's meters. I read James L. Jones's meters. I read the meters at the Hollywood Bowl. If you lived in L.A. at that time, I likely read your meters too.

While I was always on the move, speed-walking from meter to meter—jumping fences, leaping over brick walls, cutting through a whole residential street's worth of backyards—I still had a lot of time to think. And what I thought about entailed a kind of rhyming—squaring the experience of hard, blue-collar work against my liberal arts college courses in Shakespeare, British and American Romanticism, Chinese and Japanese literature, and the philosophy of Ludwig Wittgenstein. What I didn't want to do was isolate one experience from the other. What I wanted was to *join* my life—one of work along the wide and narrow avenues of L.A.—to the great voices I was hearing in my head as I traipsed, in 95-degree heat, up a long hill full of apartment houses, dodging children and dogshit along the sidewalks. *They flee from me that sometime did me seek* would echo in my mind as I glanced from behind a lavish bush of jasmine flowers, its redolent scent carried on an ocean breeze, over a magnificent patch of the aquamarine Pacific pitching in cowlicks of waves below me.

On a given day, I'd take my lunch in a park I'd spotted on my route, opening up my sack of sandwiches, chips, and cut cucumbers and carrots. I'd have time for gazing deeply from under the mottled shade of a bigleaf maple tree out toward the end of whatever block to a confusion of billboards, street traffic, fast-food joints, and the sheen of yellow and brown along the belly of sky above them. I'd see past these to Othello standing under stars, raging in his folly; to Ophelia recumbent in a coffin of pond water; to lunatic Whitman yawping in ecstatic praise for all our peoples under democratic vistas.

I had that job over five or six summers. I liked it. It gave me a rhythm for my thoughts. It gave me the acquaintance of all of Los Angeles and its harbor. It gave me the start to all further ramblings and the groundnotes to a barbaric song of knowings to come.

In the Charles Wright Museum

In the late spring of 1981, the skies were always a light azure blue during most of the days in Southern California, cypresses camphored out their scent from around the swimming pool below my living room window, and the soft green prisms of aspen leaves would spin and quake on all the small trees over the walkways of my apartment house. I was a graduate student at UC Irvine, living with my girlfriend Cynthia in a two-bedroom upstairs unit in Costa Mesa—yellow shag carpet, stacked orange crates for bookshelves and room dividers, a gaudy sectional sofa I found at a swap meet, a huge hand-me-down Panasonic TV, avocado green Melmac plates and yard-sale tableware, my parents' old Formica kitchen table, and a king-size mattress on the bedroom floor. The neighborhood around me was nondescript California suburban—mixed ranch homes and gigantic apartment complexes, a ball field behind a windbreak of eucalyptus trees near the thoroughfare, burrito stand behind home plate, and a strip mall on the main drag that led to the 405 and Costa Mesa freeways. You could smell the Pacific sometimes, as Newport Beach was just down the bluff, and you could hear commercial jets roaring overhead, too, as we were just under the landing and takeoff paths of the John Wayne Airport about five miles away. Nights, heavy dual-rotors from school-bus-sized Chinook CH-47 helicopters at El Toro Marine Base thwocked across the skies as the stars glowed only faintly, drowned in a luminous ambience from all the city lights.

One day, Charles Wright, recently my teacher, telephoned me to ask if I would house-sit his place in Laguna Beach while he and his wife Holly and son Luke went to their cabin in Montana for the summer. They'd be gone about eight weeks, he said, and I'd need to let him know pretty soon. Though I'd already gotten my MFA from Irvine in 1980, I was still there because I'd stayed on to enter its PhD program in Critical Theory. When Charles called me, I was just finishing up my first year, buffeted by the mental tumult of colliding theories and poetics—Longinus, Immanuel Kant, Kenneth Burke, and Jacques Derrida.

To seal the deal, Charles asked if I'd come for dinner and bring Cynthia, who was later to be my first wife. I'd never been to Charles's place before as, when he was my teacher, he was an extremely private person, seeing us students in class and maybe at afternoon poetry readings and the brief wine-and-cheese receptions at school. I'd occasionally spot him loping across campus in that easy gait of his or see him in my rearview pulling up behind me in his blue VW bug as we both hurried home to try to beat the traffic flow away from the university in the late afternoons. Slim, a bit under six feet, with wavy brown hair he wore fashionably longish, just over the ears, he looked a bit like Peter Fonda in photo-gray glasses and a brown sports coat over a dress shirt, jeans, and cowboy boots. Ever casual, he was also distant if not remote. To get to his office at school, you had to go through the main office of the English and Comparative Literature Department, which locked its doors during the lunch hour, and, oddly, he had once scheduled his office hours to coincide. It seemed to me that, most of the time, Charles was in a world all his own and that he liked it.

I got directions from Charles over the phone and, about a week later, Cynthia and I drove down Pacific Coast Highway to Laguna Beach, then and now certainly a part of what's called "the California Riviera." I'd been to Laguna many times, but only for part of a day or an evening, sporting in the tide pools with friends from college, once taking a date to see Kirk Douglas play McMurphy in a stage version of *One Flew Over the Cuckoo's Nest* at the Laguna Playhouse. But I'd never been to the "Top of the World," the ridgeline neighborhood near where Charles's house was—up a long incline that wound up the steep hillside above the town. Charles's place was just below the top of the Top, off on a dead-end street along a short shelf bulldozed into the earth with a huge vacant hillside field next to it, a gigantic pepper tree drooping over the asphalt driveway as we pulled up. Holly called from behind an opened window where she stooped over the kitchen sink, rinsing salad greens. Cynthia and I got out of my battered Toyota Corolla and stepped across the drive, the litter of pepper pods snapping and grinding under our feet.

Behind some shrubs and a hanging pot of purple and pink fuchsias, Charles was out on the front deck, waving at us, standing over the half-globe of a Weber BBQ, grilling kebobs of veggies and sliced sausages, smoke and sizzle rising in the billows of air around him. Luke, a blond boy of about ten I'd guessed, stood nearby, holding a long, ropelike loop of another sausage ready to throw on the grill. A cat, black with white socks and a harlequin's tragicomic face, groomed itself by the trunk of a pepper tree that grew through a hole on the other side of the deck. Holly came out and set the table, saying we'd be eating outside, *al fresco*, the first time I'd heard the phrase I think. She laid out gorgeous cobalt-blue water goblets, big plates of glazed pottery (each with its own pattern), and thick stainless tableware. The deck furniture was of a kind I'd seen in movies— "knockoff Brown-Jordan," Charles calls it in a poem—and there was a parasol awning drawn shut in the far corner of the deck. You could see the Pacific, like a blue-green sheet with embroideries of white combers stretching out below us. And, until Holly asked Charles to shut it off, I heard a shush of sprinklers dousing all the vines of ivy, vinca blossoms, and pumpkin blooms surrounding the deck, like a raft in a sea of botanicals. I knew this was another world.

After dinner, Charles and Holly took us through the U-shaped layout of the ranch-style house, showing us the whats and wheres, urging us to use everything "except the VW, which I'd appreciate if you'd start up now and again," Charles said, standing in the open garage near a huge California oak tree out back. He opened an old white refrigerator he kept back there. More than three dozen green- and bronze-colored bottles—Heinekens and St. Pauli Girls—gleamed under the brisk fridge light within and a half-dozen bottles of a light amber-colored Italian white wine. "Drink as much as you like," he said, "and don't worry about putting any more back." Through that summer, I minded him, acquiring a taste for Santa Margherita Pinot Grigio, now nearly $30 a bottle, then less than $4 per. But Heineken I never did take to, preferring a St. Pauli Girl now and again.

Inside, Charles showed us the leather-bound, two-volume Samuel Johnson *Dictionary* stacked on a secretary in the living room. From a bookcase built into its wall, he pulled out a few books he recommended I read—*The Book of Laughter and Forgetting* and *The White Hotel* among them—but none poetry. Under our feet was a lavish, indigo blue Chinese rug spread over the dark, hardwood floors. There were phoenixes in each corner of it, a bordering of pink lotus flowers, and it was mainly of a color I'd never seen on fabric before, but only in deep, Pacific waters. The ocean itself and the orange glaze of sky over it were visible through the large picture window over a camelback sofa upholstered in pearlescent white brocade. Charles showed me his liquor chest—just an old, hinged wooden box on the floor—and small stack of LPs leaning beside it. He showed me the sugar chest they used for a coffee table. He walked me through the TV room—a small den with a bearskin rug and battered leather recliner. He said to "just mail the mail" in SASEs he'd prepared and that he'd appreciate my paying the utility bills and he'd pay me back right away. Except for his being my teacher and the place having its elegant touches, it all seemed pretty normal and straightforward. Cynthia and I would be caretakers of a kind, I realized, and we'd enjoy the spaciousness, the huge quiet I felt up here, the bucolic surroundings. And maybe I'd finally get some poems written after a long year as a PhD student having written none. Of course I said *Yes.*

In 1978, before I moved back to SoCal, where I'd grown up as a teenager in Gardena and gone to college in Claremont, I'd been living in Seattle and running an Asian American community theater group I'd named "The Asian Exclusion Act" after the anti-Asian immigration and land ownership laws of the nineteenth and twentieth centuries. I applied to Irvine because I'd wanted to study with Charles Wright. I'd just read *China Trace*, his fourth book and one I thought understood the deep spiritualism in the Chinese practice of landscape poetry. I'd been introduced to poems of the T'ang Dynasty (618–907 AD) through the translations of Kenneth Rexroth and a class in Chinese literature (in translation) I took as an undergraduate at Pomona College. I'd even written my own imitations of Chinese poems. But Wright's were of a different order altogether. They had the snap and surface roughness of the contemporary, yet connected at the core with a great, still voice of calm that I associated with T'ang mysticism and dignity. And they were beautiful as the River of Stars.

Clear Night

Clear night, thumb-top of a moon, a back-lit sky.
Moon-fingers lay down their same routine.
On the side deck and the threshold, the white keys and the
    black keys.
Bird hush and bird song. A cassia flower falls.

I want to be bruised by God.
I want to be strung up in a strong light and singled out.
I want to be stretched, like music wrung from a dropped
    seed.
I want to be entered and picked clean.

And the wind says "What?" to me.
And the castor beans, with their little earrings of death, say
    "What?" to me.
And the stars start out on their cold slide through the dark.
And the gears notch and the engines wheel.
    (from *China Trace*)

When I got a call from Charles, inviting me to come to study in the MFA program at Irvine, I could hardly believe my luck. It was early spring in Seattle and the cherries were just starting to bloom, their blossoms sometimes skittering in the wind amidst the light flurries of snowflakes that looked just like them. Charles on the phone sounded like Southern Comfort tasted—smooth, slow, and sweet—like the voices of country singers I'd heard on TV. Even when they spoke, they seemed to warble. I hadn't expected him to sound so . . . *Tennessee!* But I loved it.

In workshops, though, Charles was rarely the most talkative. He was, instead, probably the most taciturn, sitting with us in the workshop circle, presiding while others held forth. Ever gentle, he'd make a small suggestion here and there, saying wise and pithy things like, "The short line depends on the image, the long line on rhythmic integrity," "This poem of yours ends before it ends, you know?" and, "Many are chosen, few are called." I recall he'd raised his voice only once, during my first year, after a guy in the workshop had been excoriating me for sentimentality, accusing me of derivative surrealism regarding a particular poem. In it, I'd described pears ripening on the kitchen windowsill as having "smooth, wide hips / freckled like a woman's" or some such extravagance. The man ended his rant by saying, "C'mon! Pears don't have hips!" Charles roared back, "Oh, *YES* they do!" His vehemence, completely uncharacteristic, ended the critique, and the group moved on. I've loved him ever since.

In the house that first night, after unloading our things—a few boxes of books, some cassette tapes, a Sony boom box, our clothes, Cynthia's violin and sheet music, my Smith-Corona typewriter—Cynthia and I walked around as though we were in a museum, padding softly from room to room. Without Charles, Holly, and Luke there, the place seemed a relic of their living— the rooms so uninhabited, the Victorian wingback chairs in the living room vacant of their bodies, the wood-paneled walls and ceiling of the hallway between the bedrooms so close and claustrophobic. There were too many picture frames hanging on the walls and propped up on tables, dressers, and nightstands. And the sepiaed people in them seemed so ancient, handsome, and unlike us. Strangers to this house and not of its family, feeling their rawboned stares boring in on us, we blessed them and turned each one over. A moth danced through an opened window (there were no screens, as Charles and Holly would have nothing interfere with a view) and fluttered through the dining room and kitchen. A pyramid of light from a brass lamp lit half a corner of the living room and the moth found it, rattling and tapping itself to tatters, while wraiths rose from the floorboards and floated by the sugar chest.

> The dead are waiting for us in our rooms,
> Little globules of light
> In one of the far corners, and close to the ceiling, hovering,
> > thinking our thoughts.

Often they'll reach a hand down,
Or offer a word, and ease us out of our bodies to join them
    in theirs.
We look back at our selves on the bed.
    (from "Homage to Paul Cézanne" in *The Southern Cross*)

We fell asleep in Charles and Holly's bed, lying down where they
had lain down, in our own nightclothes but within the narrow
shadows of their bodies enfolding us through the cool night.

I awakened and sat bolt upright in bed, staring into the dark,
hearing the chorus of crickets and frogs outside, the shush of
a car's tires on the winding road down the hill, and the kind of
thing I might have called a voice if I had to put a name to it. It
was like a ghost, tasking me—or the *not*-me:

Hand that lifted me once, lift me again,
Sort me and flesh me out, fix my eyes.
From the mulch and the undergrowth, protect me and pass
    me on.
From my own words and my certainties,
From the rose and the easy cheek, deliver me, pass me on.
    (from "Self-Portrait" in *The Southern Cross*)

I fell back asleep, sensing the shadows that rocked in the back-
yard by the oak tree, that sailed overhead huge in the night sky,
turning with the zodiac, bestowing their unction upon the bas-
kets of silk in the corners of the borrowed bedroom.

Holy Thursday

Begins with the *ooo ooo* of a mourning dove
In the pepper tree, crack
Of blue and a flayed light on the hills,
Myself past the pumpkin blooms and out in the disked field,
Blake's children still hunched in sleep, dollops
Of bad dreams and an afterlife,
Canticles rise in spate from the bleeding heart.
Cathedrals assemble and disappear in the water beads.
I scuff at the slick adobe, one eye
On the stalk and one on the aftermath.
    (from "Holy Thursday" in *The Southern Cross*)

The cooing of mourning doves in the eaves outside the bedroom window woke me, and I roused myself that first morning, feeling half inside a netherworld, pulling myself up by the roots, trying to leave it. Charles's poem for William Blake, the visionary Romantic who wrote *Songs of Innocence and Songs of Experience*, flashed through me like a ladderlight I could climb from here to where Blake might be, where Charles was, warbling to me from the other side of things. It was damn weird. I was inside one of my teacher's poems. I threw on some jeans and a T-shirt and walked out into the living room, hoping Cynthia would have put the coffee on.

She had, but was already outside on the deck, laying out toast and jellies, fruit, and coffee—a miracle for breakfast!—on the outdoor table. The deck was littered with fuchsia blossoms that I kicked and crushed as I walked over. I saw a gray light glinting off the Pacific, tufts of fog creeping up the vacant lot on the hillside next to the property, and heard a strange hush covering everything except the tinkle of glasses and a cup set down on a saucer. Cynthia hummed a melody from Brahms as she poured me coffee. A mockingbird twittered and piped from some tree across the driveway.

> The hawk realigns herself.
> Splatter of mockingbird notes, a brief trill from the jay.
> The fog starts in, breaking its various tufts loose.
> Everything smudges and glows,
> Cactus, the mustard plants and the corn [. . .]
>
> Surf sounds in the palm tree,
> Sussurations, the wind
>   making a big move from the west,
> The children asleep again, their second selves
> Beginning to stir [. . .]
> From under the billowing dead, from their wet hands and a
>   saving grace,
> The children begin to move, an angle of phosphorescence
> Along the ridge line.
>   (from "Holy Thursday")

All around me were Charles's lines and his poems—his deck, the shrubs and flowers, the weather and hillside, and the Pacific below were all characters and figures in his own lyric dramas.

Sun like an orange mousse through the trees,
A snowfall of trumpet bells on the oleander;
                                                    mantis paws
Craning out of the new wisteria; fruit smears in the west . . .
DeStael knifes a sail on the bay;

[. . .]

A wing brushes my left hand,
                                    but it's not my wing.
    (from "Dog Day Vespers" in *The Southern Cross*)

Laguna Beach was the stage for Charles's post-Romantic epic, albeit a skeptical one, of salvation and redemption. I'd stumbled straight into his Paradiso, each scene surrounding me an illustrative panel of his somber and sometimes wacky devotion to pursuing spiritual questions in our time. It was a drag. Where could I look where Charles had not? What could I find in the images around me to capture and make due service for my own poems? He not only owned every spoon and flyswatter, he owned the very trees, highway mirages, and camphorous orbs of light wherever I looked. I sensed a tough summer ahead.

Giving up, I worked on an essay about poetry instead of trying to write it. I'd made an "Incomplete" for one of my graduate classes—the result of catching pneumonia that winter for lack of sleep and the subsequent stress on my system. There was so much to read and understand—the philosophic texts of John Locke and René Descartes along with *Lyrical Ballads* and Wallace Stevens's "Sunday Morning," psychoanalytic essays by Jacques Lacan and the dizzying writings of Jacques Derrida, the prima ballerina of something called deconstruction. I gave up sleep and got sick and had a major seminar paper to write as makeup. I cleared my mind of the philosophic babble in my head and wrote a pedestrian piece of literary appreciation on Derek Walcott, the grand poet from the island of Saint Lucia in the Caribbean.

> And here's a line of brown ants cleaning a possum's skull,
> And here's another, come from the opposite side.
>   (from "Dead Color" in *The Other Side of the River*)

Ants were everywhere. On the kitchen windowsills, across the counters, emerging from under the floorboards and electric duplexes in the walls. They marched in a thick, writhing line from the deck, over the transom of the front door, and into the living room, over the Chinese rug and up onto a lampstand to a box, covered in butcher paper, which had come in the mail. It was from the poet Mark Jarman, addressed to Charles, and stamped *FRAGILE* and *DO NOT FORWARD*. The ants were streaming under its tightly creased folds and swarming to something they liked inside of it.

Younger than me by a year, Mark had been a teacher of mine in the Irvine program too, coming during my second year, fresh from an NEA grant to Italy and maybe only a couple years out from his own MFA at Iowa. I'd known his work from long before and loved it for how it rendered, with insouciance and rhetorical panache, the typical teenager's life in Redondo Beach, California. His early poems, published in the most thrilling lit mags of our time while we were still undergraduates—*kayak, Antaeus,* and even *Poetry*—had titles like "Making Out with the Ghosts of Old Girlfriends" and chronicled prom nights and cruising Pacific Coast Highway on Friday nights, mentioned surfing and football, and mocked the angry, protective father (of a girl he'd French kissed) who flung a handful of gravel on the roof of his car while he sped away, cackling like the Fonz leaning into the wheel of his '57 Chevy. That Jarman could sure write some shit and, *gavacho* or not, he knew who we were—the Chicanos, bloods, and Buddhas on his high school football team. I respected him.

But the ants marching into the house and munching on something inside of that package scared me. What the hell had he sent to Charles anyway? I called him.

116

It was popcorn. Jarman had gotten some from a packing out-fit in Murray, Kentucky, where he taught, placed a gift in a ship-ping box, and then filled it with the stuff. The ants were going for that.

"Just take the mounted photograph out of the box, empty out all the popcorn, and you'll be rid of those ants," Jarman said, detailed and procedural as a TV pathologist.

I did so and pulled, from inside the boxful of ant-bearded puffs, a picture of a series of photographed butterfly wings. The ornate patterns corresponded to letters and spelled out a line from a poem of Theodore Roethke's: *All finite things reveal infinitude.*

The Wrights's cat was a hunter. We were to feed it from a big plastic tub of cat food stored on the back porch along with the stinking cat box, but it still liked to hunt things. One morning while I was reading, it padded in from outside up to the edge of the Chinese rug, carrying something gray in its mouth, then dropped it onto the deep blue, expansive infield of the carpet. It was a mockingbird, its head askew, one wing tucked up under its limp carcass, the other splayed out and reaching for a lotus flower floating on the rug's border nearby. When I didn't react, the cat snatched at it with a paw so its head bobbled. A wing rustled briefly against the carpet, then was still forever. The cat opened its jaws in a wide, whiskered yawn and purred. *Splatter of mockingbird notes, a brief trill from the jay.*

Winter Wright, Charles's brother, called one afternoon. "I want-ed to know if he got that pen I sent for his birthday," he said. Later, talking to Charles, giving him one of my biweekly reports (he'd driven from his cabin out to some pay phone at a cross-roads near Kalispell, Montana), he said, "Oh, my brother always gives me a pen." So blasé. Winter Wright, I knew from an inter-view that ran in *Field*, a poetry magazine from Oberlin College where Charles published a lot, was named after their mother's family name. And she was sister to the father of Johnny and Ed-gar Winter, blues musicians from Texas that I've adored since I was in high school. I found Charles's copy of that first epony-mous Johnny Winter album, a Columbia LP, leaned up against the liquor cabinet, mixed in with about an arm's length worth of records. Among them were recordings from the Carter Family, Johnny Cash, Bach's "Goldberg Variations" by Glenn Gould, and the first two albums from The Band. Country, roots rock, and Baroque piano music. And the Winter brothers. Beside a box of Jack Daniels, Smirnoff, and Wild Turkey.

We invited people over for meals. . . .

My parents and brother came down from Gardena one Sunday afternoon, I think, for a barbecue like Charles and Holly had thrown for Cynthia and me. But I substituted chicken teriyaki and *musubi* (rice balls) for the sausage kebobs and garlic bread the Wrights had fed us. The salad and beers were the same. My mother moved very little while she was there, sitting stiffly in a patio chair ("knockoff Brown-Jordan") and glancing around disapprovingly. She would not go into the house. My brother Eldon stripped to swimming trunks and sunned himself all afternoon lying on the chaise on the decks, bees nestling in the bells and blooms nearby, crows perching and taking off from a telephone wire strung almost parallel to the hazy line of the horizon. I remember that my father just grinned and ate silently. He was hard of hearing and never said much at meals. He brought his Sony transistor radio with its tiny earpiece and tuned in to replays of the stretch calls at Hollywood Park.

"Your teacher must be a fuss-budget," my mother finally proclaimed, with annoyance, after we'd all finished eating. She held her purse tightly—it was still in her lap. "His place looks fussy."

Angels
Are counting cadence, their skeletal songs
What the hymns say, the first page and the last.
(from "Holy Thursday")

Two classmates from college came over another night. We talked up a storm, they telling me of their escapades as graduate students—one at Berkeley, another at UCSD—sleeping with other students, sleeping with profs, picking up sailors in a bar and sleeping with them on the beach. There was an affair one of them had with a famous critic, who would not admit he was gay. And so on. They had both just come out and, I think,

118

wanted to shock me. But I knew who they were—sweet, short, lower middle-class SoCal boys who were scared just like me we wouldn't make it as legit literati. We consumed a couple bottles of Santa Margherita and the two six-packs of generic beer they'd brought. The fog was thick outside when they left. I could hear their car with its rattling muffler clattering down the hillside, its gears grinding like teeth in a worried man's sleep.

> And the stars start out on their cold slide through the dark.
> And the gears notch and the engines wheel.
>   (from "Clear Night")

I realized I wasn't free, that what I wanted from my own writing might be silly compared to what I was being guided through— the poemscape of Charles Wright's visionary world. I had to relinquish will, renounce my own plans, and accept this journey I was being taken on, each item around me—every leaf, every flower, every birdcall and shine of light in the trees, every cymbal splash and gut-thunk from the kickdrum of the rock-and-roll band practicing in a garage down the street was curated, an icon in the Charles Wright Museum and Gardens where I was the caretaker that summer.

> Some nights, when the rock-and-roll band next door has quit
>   playing,
> And the last helicopter has thwonked back to the Marine
>   base,
> And the dark lets all its weight down
>   to within a half inch of the ground,
> I sit outside in the gold lamé of the moon
>   as the town sleeps and the country sleeps
> Like flung confetti around me,
> And wonder just what in the hell I'm doing out here
> So many thousands of miles away from what I know best.
> And what I know best
>   has nothing to do with Point
>   Conception
> And Avalon and the long erasure of ocean
> Out there where the landscape ends.
> What I know best is a little thing.

It sits on the far side of the simile,
                        the like that's like the like.
        (from "California Dreaming" in *The Other Side of the River*)

Those first weeks in Charles's house, as the quiet and bucolics
got hold of me, as a willow tree let down its spiny green lattices
before my eyes, his poems were like dragon's teeth in Ovid's
Metamorphoses. Strewn over seemingly vacant ground, they rose
up like soft skeletal cages, closing me in, trapping me as I tried
to fight against them with the broad swords of my own strophes.
But they were myriads—orioles shuttling and weaving in the
trees, the squawk from a jay, jonquils and jasmine around the
deck, houseflies and gnats that zigzagged within a shady column
of gloom inside the house. Within weeks, I gave in to these bril-
liant cages of my surroundings, and their spaces conjoined into
a vast, sectional aviary and expanded into an arboretum I wan-
dered within, encountering Where the Sublime Things Are.

Wu-wei, I thought then, the Chinese Taoist principle of "let-
ting be." And once I could do that, the poems unfurled for me,
their images like small pellets of colored paper that, if placed in
a bowl of water, bloomed into lavish flowers of artifice and imag-
ination. The "Darvon dustfall off the Pacific" that Charles de-
scribed was a stunning gateway into his memories—of childhood
and adolescence in Tennessee, driving winding country roads
across the county line to fetch a bottle of gin with his brother;
sitting on bricks of a walkway in Venice, letting his legs dangle
and watching the ochre reflections of a palazzo glint, wither, and
resurrect on the crepuscular surface of a canal's lapping waters;
laughing with Army buddies in a Florentine bar; witnessing the
"spiked marimbas of dawn rattling their amulets" on a Dantes-
can hillside in Hawai'i. And then each of these turned to a deep-
er, more esoteric and ephemeral meditation—the product of
his observations and abundant quietudes, as Charles says, "the
far side of the simile / the like that's like the like." The poems
are reflections not only of the earth and its properties, the mind
and its acts of affectionate and somber memory, but conclusions
and speculations regarding insubstantial things—the ghosts and
frail gods interfused in an infinite, trans-substantial music that
were the actual subjects of the man's work. Inside his poems,

living as I was in a museum and the attached botanical gardens of his words, I traveled with him through the creation around me, to memory and its attendant regrets and joys, to minute and everlasting confrontations with the Absolute.

I got to poking around. On the far side of the house, back around the rear porch, a closet for the hot water tank, a huge California oak tree, and down a narrow gutter of concrete for drainage, I discovered a small, locked room the size of a closet for garden tools. My house key didn't open it. But there was a window to one side of its door. And an old, rotting screen, cloaked in silt, was in front of it. I'd been out back watering Holly's flowers and had wandered down to where the hose was hooked up or got hung up. But somehow I drifted down there, beside the great god of the disked, hillside field, patchy with oat grass, that stretched from below the dead-end of the street and up to the ridgeline above Charles's house.

When I peeked inside, I saw a black-and-white photo of an oval-faced man, his eyes clenched shut. The face was wizened, half-shaved and with an unkempt goatee. It was Ezra Pound, the great Modernist poet who'd tutored T. S. Eliot and championed Robert Frost early on, then became a Fascist living in Italy, supporting Mussolini and going on the air over the radio, denouncing America and the Allies in odd rants about economics. But he was also a great poet of expansive remorse and a documentarian of literary and visual beauties, writing "The Pisan Cantos" from the outdoor cage where he was imprisoned for a time after the end of World War II.

What thou lovest well remains,
the rest is dross
What thou lov'st well shall not be reft from thee
What thou lov'st well is thy true heritage . . .
   Ezra Pound, Canto LXXXI

Pound was one of Charles's heroes, I knew, as he'd quoted Pound a few times in workshops ("Poetry consists of piths and gists," E. P., *The ABC of Reading*), was inspired by him, and invoked him in his own poems:

121

I remember the way that Pound walked
                              across San Marco
At *passeggiata*, as though with no one,
                          his eyes on the long ago.
(from "The Southern Cross" in *The Southern Cross*)

I gathered the photo of Pound was a postcard and then, as
my eyes adjusted to the shadows, I realized that the entire wall
inside was covered with postcards, photographs, and bits of
things pinned to it. I ran back inside the house and fetched a
flashlight from the kitchen. I got back to the window of the little
room, snicked on the slide-switch piggy-backed on the barrel of
the light, and shone it like a probe inside the dark. There were
postcards of a Baroque Christian cross, the Ponte Vecchio in
Florence, a fresco panel by Masaccio, a few flowers, a black mask
for carnival, and photographs of Charles himself as a younger
man (unsmiling) lying sideways behind a row of pumpkins, as
a boy dressed in his Sunday best, and standing with James Tate
(his buddy from their days at the Iowa Workshop) inside the
courtyard of a Venetian palazzo. I strained and squinted, cali-
brating and focusing the movements of the yellow spot of light
hampered by the funky double-scrim of the paired screen and
window, shut one eye and pressed my face hard against it, flat-
tening screen against window glass, trying to see more of what
lay inside the murk of the room. Obvious now were a tiny sec-
retary and chair, a reporter's manual typewriter, and a piece of
scrimshaw atop a low bookcase—but there was just a half-shelf
of literary magazines and few books in it. Instead, there was a
child's single, red shoe; a tin box; animal figurines; a toy car
made of lead, small flecks of gaudy paint still clinging to its sur-
face; and shards of quartz.

I like it back here

Under the green swatch of the pepper tree and the aloe
    vera.

[. . .]

Surrounded by fetishes and figures of speech:
Dog's tooth and whale's tooth, my father's shoe, the dead
    weight
Of winter, the inarticulation of joy . . .
The spirits are everywhere.
    (from "Ars Poetica" in *The Southern Cross*)

This was Charles Wright's writing studio, of course, where he must've typed up his manuscripts, where he shut himself in from the world and gazed upon relics from his own past, touched talismans of other lives, and ran his fingers through the wing-feathers of Renaissance angels:

How I would like a mountain
                if I had means enough to live as a recluse.
I would like to renounce it all
And turn toward the ash-gold flame
                mullioned between the palm fronds.
    (from "T'ang Notebook" in *The Other Side of the River*)

About a year later, Charles published "Looking at Pictures," a gorgeous poem that catalogued all he had back in that little room. I got to calling it C. W.'s *hōjō*, invoking "The Diary of the Hut Ten-Foot Square" of the twelfth-century Japanese recluse Kamo-no-Chōmei. Chōmei lived in a shack beside the Kamo River in Kyoto and described his Diogenean retirement from the world from that humble perspective. Wright's wasn't all that different to me. His room seemed an eremite's cave of meditation filled with icons, his walls lit by flames of the spiritual.

How many times have I come here
                to look at these photographs
And reproductions of all I've thought most beautiful
In the natural world,
And tried to enter the tired bodies assembled in miniature?

St. Francis, for instance, who saw the fire in the pig's mouth,
And trees full of the drowned
                who forgot to cross themselves.
Or the last half-page of the Verse of Light in Arabic

> torn from the Koran,
> Tacked like a terrible crystal this side of the reading lamp.
> Beside it Adam and Eve in agony
> Are ushered out through the stone gates of Paradise.
> (from "Looking at Pictures" in *The Other Side of the River*)

What is there left to say after you've witnessed a poet's arrival at this kind of glory?

In another closet, this one inside the house in the far bedroom, I found a phalanx of about a dozen dry-cleaned dress shirts, all neatly pressed, starched, and hung, on wire hangers, exactly the same distance apart—about a quarter inch—as though he'd lined them up and used calipers to space them properly for dress parade. And then there were about a half-dozen jeans, hung on wood hangers, also precisely the same distance apart, each pressed and lightly starched with a hard, cleaner's crease on each pant leg. *Angels / are counting cadence, . . . / . . . the first page and the last.*

The rest of that summer I just went about my business like a janitor, flipping my keys, making my rounds, watering the plants and grounds, drinking up the boss-man's liquor. I was constantly drunk with Charles's spirit. Sometimes I'd drive down the lane away from his house, bomb down the narrow road and its moguls, race to get groceries or on some errand or other down in the town with its bustle, its aprons of surf and tide pools, then hurry on back up the hill to rest in how cool it was up at his place, how glorified the universe seemed to be as it wrote "the silvery alphabet of the sea . . ." whenever I glanced down from the deck and out to the gray sheet of the Pacific.

At the end of summer, Cynthia and I packed up our things into U-Haul boxes, fitted everything we'd brought into one carload (broke, we'd acquired nothing all summer), and drove away from my lessoning past the portable toilet parked by a half-built house down the street, under the lazy gyres of a turkey buzzard wheeling in an indeterminate apse of sky above us. Good-bye to all that.

After that summer, I gave Charles a few gifts—books I liked that were special to me and one I found that I thought might be so to him. The Chinese treasure an anthology of poetry collected during the T'ang Dynasty they simply call the *Three Hundred Poems of the T'ang* (*Tang Shi San Bai Shou*). I found a copy of it in a bookshop in L.A. Chinatown. Published in Taipei, it had orange paper covers and the image of a yellow fan across the front, with the title in both Chinese and English written in calligraphy across the folds of the fan. I didn't recognize the translation, but I liked it a lot as I browsed. I bought two copies and gave one to Charles as a New Year's present. In it were poems by Li Po ("the high heavenly priest of the White Lake," Charles calls him in "Portrait of the Artist with Li Po"), Tu Fu, T'ao Ch'ien, and Wang Wei—master eremites all. He gave the volume a mention in a note at the back of *The Other Side of the River*. But it bothered Charles that no translator was acknowledged. Later, he told me he'd figured out that it was a bootleg of *The Jade Mountain*, Witter Bynner's lovely 1929 English version of this great book. I also gave him a copy of Donald Keene's translations of Yoshida Kenkō's *Essays in Idleness* (*Tsurezuregusa*), a kind of diary of an aesthete from the fourteenth century in Japan. Later, I found a few lines about Kenkō in one of Charles's poems:

It's true, I think, as Kenkō says in his *Idleness*,
That all beauty depends on disappearance,
The bitten edges of things,
       the gradual sliding away
Into tissue and memory,
     the uncertainty
And dazzling impermanence of days we beg our meanings
  from
And their frayed loveliness.
  (from "Lonesome Pine Special" in *The Other Side of the
  River*)

I think the last present I ever gave Charles was an old hardbound copy of *The Sacred Harp* I found at a yard or library sale on Balboa Peninsula. It's that book of shape-note singing—hymns and spirituals for church services. The lyrics were printed above notations in a kind of Western cuneiform of images making up a mnemonic lexicon of musical notes corresponding to a simple, seven-note scale. Always performed *a capella*, it was a tradition of choral singing that sprung up in the South for country folk who couldn't read music and for churches that couldn't afford a piano or organ. "All you need is faith," is what I remember Elmer Gantry, Levon Helm, or Curtis Mayfield preaching somewhere.

But what Charles had given me was as insubstantial as wisdom. "You've got to sign your name to something, it seems to me," he writes, around that time I lived in his Laguna Beach house, in a lazy-lined poem someplace in his *oeuvre*. And "Everyone's life is the same life / if you live long enough." And so his life and its memories became mine, each time I entered his poems. His Italy and its splendors became my Italy—like his remembrance in "The Southern Cross" of a drive around Lake Garda, noticing almond blossoms floating on the waves, flashing in the sun's flare like "a small flotilla of matches." His Dante and Can Grande mine, and where they stood, shadow selves within his own boot-heels digging into the ground of the Giusti Gardens, so I felt I could stand too, poet manqué, and gaze across the mists over the Adige at "the secret light Campana saw," where "Catullus once sat through the afternoons." His sadness and regrets mine, his precision of seeing and saying nearly mine—or at least I once thought so before the spell of that summer ended and my own banked fires burned again. But even living within my own ambitions, Charles had something to say to me. To him who would want career over calling, he warns in "Three Poems for the New Year," "The ache for fame is a thick dust and weariness in the heart." And to himself, a little later on in the same poem, somewhat tipsy with melancholia, he says, "The ache for anything is a thick dust in the heart." When Charles Wright handles something, whether a piece of wisdom or bough of wisteria, he handles it lazily, gently, but doesn't let it go. It always comes back, with a new twist to it, with the knot it was in loosened a little but the loops still intact and readable as Virgiliana. He gets into a string of thought and works a cat's cradle out of it, then goes around the world, like a spider, "And turns it again and again until it is shining." A piece of finitude swung around the fixed stars.

The man taught me that living in dailiness is the meditation, that, Catalina being our Dantean island of reeds, the immaculate is only perceivable through the mundane, that this world of ten thousand things is linked to our deepest thoughts in an immutable and mysterious way, *a priori*, and that one's real life, lived amidst bowers or careworn as a caneworker's hands, returns beatified if only attended to in the quiet hum of an idle dreaming. *California dreaming . . . .*

III

Introduction to *Under Western Eyes*
Culture Wars in Asian America

Since the publication breakthrough of Maxine Hong Kingston's *The Woman Warrior* in 1976, an increasingly higher level of success and diversity has been emerging in Asian American literature. During the eighties, Amy Tan's novel *The Joy Luck Club* was a runaway best seller and David Henry Hwang's play *M. Butterfly* had a hugely successful run on Broadway, winning several Tony awards. Young poets like Li-Young Lee, Marilyn Chin, David Mura, John Yau, and Cathy Song rose to national prominence, winning awards and appearing in standard textbooks and anthologies. During the nineties, both Tan's novel and Hwang's play were made into commercial films, and mainstream commercial presses and regional and literary small presses have stepped up the publication of even more novels, memoirs, volumes of poetry, and collections of short stories by Asian Americans. A list of recognizable American literary names might now include those of Gish Jen, David Wong Louie, Wendy Law-Yone, Ben Fong-Torres, Sylvia Watanabe, Frank Chin, Gus Lee, Joy Kogawa, Philip Gotanda, Jessica Hagedorn, Fae Ng, and Le Ly Hayslip. Newcomer novelists Chang-rae Lee and Julie Shigekuni will be recognized very soon. Poets Li-Young Lee, David Mura, Kiyoko Mori, and myself are now publishing memoirs and autobiographies with commercial houses. It feels like a storehouse of cultural riches has been filled, and that there is a lot of literary goodwill in the cultural bank.

Yet, alongside the recent rise in prominent national publications by Asian American writers, some troubling confusions and disputes have arisen concerning the public role of the Asian American literary artist, particularly with regard to questions of politics, community, social justice, and the representation of Asians in mass culture. There is an extremely divisive cultural war going on, made visible recently by the newspapers, that has sparked debate on university campuses and served as a hot academic topic for symposia panels across the country. Structurally speaking, the war is taking place on two ostensibly different fronts—in the mainstream culture and within Asian American academic and literary communities themselves—on the one hand pitting the Asian American writer against mainstream cultural perceptions, and then, on the other, pitting the Asian American writer against a political agenda defined as organically arising from out of diverse Asian American communities. Recent events like the academic panel at the Asian American Studies Association's 1990 convention, which featured several scholars presenting papers denouncing Ronald Takaki's prize-winning book, *Strangers from a Different Shore: A History of Asian Americans*, have demonstrated that, despite what any single author might wish, this cultural war constantly engages the Asian American writer, marginalizing and censoring individual consciousness, playing out political arguments in a social arena, and absorbing the multiple meanings of any given work into oversimplified interpretive systems regarding the relationship between ethnicity and power.

There have been critics who demand that writers serve as political instruments to bring about social justice. Claiming to act as spokespersons for the Asian American community, these critics argue that Asian American literary artists have not done enough to curb or eliminate certain exotic or negative portraits of Asians in our culture. They have even gone so far as to allege that the artists themselves have perpetuated these negative images. From the mainstream front there are yet others who feel that Asian American writers have been treated well by the culture and have little reason to argue with it and no ground for advancing political critiques. I would say that many academic colleagues, white liberals, and assimilated friends have tacitly but consistently required that we writers be silent about our outrage for the dearth of that justice being visited upon our lives. I feel that *both* of these perspectives are patronizing and proprietary and work to perpetuate the twin crimes of limiting artistic freedom and infantilizing the consciousness of the Asian American writer.

The Japanese American poet David Mura once wrote an article for *Mother Jones* about the Actors' Equity protest against the casting of British Jonathan Pryce, a white male, as the Eurasian lead in the Broadway production of *Miss Saigon.* The point had to do with the fact that no Asian was given an audition for that role, that, yet again, a *white* was playing in yellowface. Mura's article also exposed the breakup of his friendships with two white artists—a painter and a poet—as a result of his arguing with them over the legitimacy of the protest. His friends argued against reverse discrimination, against affirmative action with regard to art, against Mura's classifying them as recipients of white privilege. They insisted that they themselves had experienced discrimination, that they knew what prejudice was, that he had no point to make with them regarding their social privilege, that they were *the same* as he was. They wanted to depoliticize the racial question, setting aside the issue of representation and diffusing his very political challenge to the freedom of art. But Mura would not relent, to the point that the friendships were strained past mending.

After the article was published, there was even more difficulty. Though their actual names were never used, Mura's erstwhile friends felt that their privacy had been violated, that Mura had exploited them by including the breakup of their friendship in the article. They felt betrayed. And their social group—a goodly number of liberal, white artists in Minneapolis-St. Paul—took up their cause, creating a huge burden of social pressure upon Mura, making him feel isolated, unsupported, and reviled by the very group that had been his circle in the past.

Other writers, who may have been neutral or mildly supportive of him, began to bash him publicly, speaking disparagingly of him as an "ethnic Johnny-Come-Lately," as a traitor to his white friends, as a "self-righteous convert" to radical ethnic politics who had been so mild and acceptable in the past. The criticism came from a group of local artists that was uniformly white and middle class, a group that had previously authorized his work by including him in their circle, affording him various literary opportunities, and generally paying attention to his work. His crime was not only a conversion of consciousness, say (I would describe it as actually the *development* of consciousness), but the violation of privacy among former friends, the public report of their difficult conversations, the exposure of these very delicate and powerful maneuverings around the issues of race, representation, art, and politics. Mura was ethically faulted for exposing the discussions, for revealing things and mischaracterizing positions others took. Ultimately, to my mind, he was criminalized for breaking culturally imposed and socially policed silences surrounding the issues of race and culture in our society.

There are strong taboos against this kind of silence-breaking, and they are enforced at the level of the unconscious, disguised as ethics, protected by notions of privacy, enforced socially, and suppressed within the individual psyche as the territory of the forbidden, even at the level of thought—we dismiss what we experience as "out of bounds" to the point that we often deny their occurrences even after they've erupted.

It is often this way whenever a writer breaks a culturally imposed silence. Once he protested the ventriloquism and cultural appropriation enacted in the production of *Miss Saigon*, Mura was further victimized. In attempting to suppress his protest, Mura's liberal friends were committing a kind of cultural infantilism, trying to invalidate the authority of his perceptions and perspective on the issue, failing to respect his emerging consciousness, trying to persuade him that his hurt regarding their dismissiveness of this racial and political issue was delusionary and unrealistic. Yet, Mura persisted, pursuing his point of view, reporting on these discussions, breaking the cultural silence regarding how issues of race, art, and politics are negotiated at the levels of the interpersonal and policed by social groups.

For this outspokenness, Mura had to contend not only with the loss of friendships, but with the social mechanism of ostracism and demonization that ensued. In essence, he was *shunned*—excluded from society in a manner metonymic of the Japanese American relocation itself. Moreover, he had to endure the realization that this shunning would have economic as well as social consequences. Around literary whites in the Twin Cities, he'd forever be known as a troublemaker, likely costing him consideration for an academic job, curbing his invitations to contribute to local literary publications. He became widely known for a controversial political position with regard to art, and, once he became racially identified, he was cast out of his former circle. Very rapidly, he became friends with people of color, who seemed to rally him.

Though our culture often claims that art is a separate category not entirely subject to the principles of political fairness our democracy might impose on elections and businesses, it is nearly impossible to ignore issues of representation, white privilege, and freedom of expression when we examine the images of peoples of color authorized by our culture. African Americans, Native Americans, Hispanics, and Asian Americans have long been subject to the power of the stereotype regarding their portrayals in the cultural mainstream. *Miss Saigon* is simply one of the most recent misrepresentations regarding Asians promulgated by our culture.

In protesting the producer's refusal to consider casting an Asian in the lead role, Mura opposed a long-standing tradition of white cultural privilege to represent the Other—whether Arab or black, Asian or Native American. This idea arises, perhaps, out of a primitive delight in spectacle, in seeing exotic things displayed for public delectation. It plays on cultural and psychic fear of the unknown, on susceptibilities to the sublime (dread mixed with fascination), and on the relationship between ignorance and the imagination. It is the essence of theater. Yet it falsifies, for reasons of spectacle and entertainment, the cultural and interpersonal identities of the very peoples it purports to represent.

During Shakespeare's time in England, the costumer Inigo Jones was famous for dressing actors in false beards and headdresses; in gowns, robes, and outsize pantaloons; in thick makeup and jewelry so as to create in the appearance that they were Moors, Jews, and Spaniards. The plays and masques of Renaissance England took white actors and created Orientals and Indians, blackamoors and rajas, gypsies and khans. In nineteenth-century America, white singers and dancers engaged in the practice of blackening their faces to make farcical the illusion that they were black minstrels. In this way, white performers colonized an African American tradition for white audiences, furthering the European tradition of white displacement, substitution, and usurpation of the ethnic in cultural practice. Later, during the 1920s, white musicians copied the styles and took the innovations of African Americans from New Orleans and made a reputation as musical originators themselves. Al Jolson—a Jewish entertainer—then made blackface an American icon in *The Jazz Singer*, the first "talkie," a motion picture with recorded dialogue, made in the late 1920s. In the silent film *Broken Blossoms*, a story of forbidden love between the races, a white actor played a tragic Chinese. Charlie Chan, the Chinese detective of the 1930s and '40s movie serials, was always played by a white actor in makeup that made him appear slant-eyed. During and shortly after World War II, English-speaking Chinese and Korean actors started appearing in American commercial films like *Back to Bataan* and *The Flying Tigers* as Japanese military villains— more realistic updates of Ming the Merciless, a thirties pulp fiction and comic book character who was brutal, clever, and completely maleficent. The stereotype was again transformed in the 1950s, when white actors Marlon Brando and Mickey Rooney played slurred speech, buck-toothed Asian males in movies like *Teahouse of the August Moon* and *Breakfast at Tiffany's*. Brando's Sakini was a sidekick buffoon, a procurer and helpmate to Glenn Ford's lead, a Caucasian army officer stationed in postwar Okinawa. Rooney's character was the salacious Japanese landlord to ingénue Audrey Hepburn. He suggested sexual favors in lieu of rent. Sexual threat to white women, emasculation, physical brutality, and social buffoonery are all part of the Asian male presence in American popular culture.

The stereotype was thus so firmly in place that, when television began to portray Asians, the characters, this time played by *Asian* actors, had to conform. *Bachelor Father*, a half-hour comedy series, featured a Korean cook who spoke in fractured English and wrote indecipherable notes to star Jon Forsyth in a kind of pidgin phonetics. *Bonanza*, an NBC western, had its Chinaman, Hop Sing, yelling to the Cartwrights, his masters, in mixed Cantonese and chop-suey English. Thus, first-generation Asian

American creoles became identified with farce and buffoonery, invalidating the heroic languages of our pioneering ancestors.

Historically, the image of the Other produced by mainstream culture has flattered white supremacy, diminished ethnic dignity, masked the ethnic origins of certain art forms (i.e., jazz), and usurped creative opportunities for ethnics to represent themselves in a manner independent of the operating stereotypes. There is a tradition of *mis*representation with regard to the Other, and people of color sense it acutely, particularly when confronted with new outbreaks and hugely popular manifestation it such as *Miss Saigon*, where the usurpation and stereotyping is so blatant. We have been appearing, for far too long, under Western eyes.

I once struggled with a similar issue when reviewing Gretel Ehrlich's novel *Heart Mountain* for the *New York Times Book Review* in 1988. The novel's setting is the concentration camp in Wyoming that housed 18,000 Japanese Americans during World War II. The principal characters are four Japanese Americans and the ranchers, sheepmen, waitresses, and itinerant cowboys of the area. The hero is a white rancher who falls in love and has an affair with a beautiful Japanese American woman who is a painter educated in Paris. But she is married—to a Nisei who beats her, a political dissident who rages against the government and its racist policies. The other two main Japanese American male characters are benign and ineffectual—the painter's kindly father who carves Noh masks and seems to approve of his daughter's extramarital affair and a young reporter for the camp newspaper who masturbates nightly, fantasizing her body joining with his.

In my review I pointed out that the Japanese American male characters are portrayed as menacing, emasculated, or mystically benign while the principal Japanese American female character is portrayed as lissome and exotic, sexually available to whites. I said this was still the production of the Other, that Ehrlich's novel, however well-intentioned and politically sympathetic, still suffered from unconscious stereotyping and some historical ignorance regarding the Japanese American characters and their experiences. I found it unreasonable to condemn the book, as I enjoyed its narrative flow and its affecting portraits of ranch life. Yet, in good conscience, I had to raise an objection regarding what I felt to be an almost laughably racist treatment of its Japanese American characters. My criticism came in a single paragraph in a review that, overall, praised the book for its portrait of Wyoming ranch life and its aesthetic loyalties to a magnificent landscape.

During the year that followed, I was occasionally accused (most prominently by a white female Pulitzer Prize winner) of having acted like an "ethnic hit man," policing the work of white writers who dared to approach treating the lives of people of color. I was characterized as holding to the "politically correct" position that a white writer could not and *should not* write about people of color, that a white writer should not presume to speak *on behalf* of oppressed peoples, that a white writer who did so was colonizing the experiences of minorities who should be allowed to speak for themselves. This criticism was itself an act of cultural ventriloquism, as my published position asserted nothing of the kind. A system of cultural fear, a complicated manifestation of backlash, had appropriated my review and recharacterized me as radically ethnocentric. Somehow, the report of literary gossip held more authority than the printed words themselves.

Here, my own experience mirrored Mura's in the aftermath of his *Mother Jones* piece. The reactions in both are typical of a society based upon an idea of cultural "centering" that unconsciously appropriates the experiences of racial minorities and interprets for them what their identities and consciousnesses shall be. When this process is criticized, particularly by anyone considered to be a racial or cultural "Other," the culture erupts in a backlash that takes a variety of forms, ranging from social shunning to active discreditation and persecution. Cultural conservatives perceive both the critique and the presentation of alternative interpretations as a threat to cultural stability and their own prestige. The view from the center is powerfully resistant to the incorporation of diversity, to any attempt to "de-center" its primary aesthetic and cultural beliefs about itself (e.g., that "culture" itself is universal and is empowered to absorb, flatten, and erase political and racial differences). The writer who comes from the margin, from minority enclave communities, from suppressed histories, from lifestyles not in the mainstream of society, generally has an extremely difficult time persuading audiences—even an audience of intimates who might share the same suppressed histories—that presentation of the new narratives brought to our culture by critical voices, often of minorities and women, is beneficial and not as destabilizing as so many feel it is. To speak *about* a trauma or social prohibition, to speak against silencing, can initiate further acts of trauma, silencing, and prohibition of the speaker.

For example, most adult Americans now seem willing to acknowledge the injustice of the Japanese American relocation during World War II. In 1989, Congress made a kind of national festival of its formal, legislative apology to those who had suffered internment, creating an entitlement program to make a small financial redress for every living survivor of the internment. But this was not always the case. Not too long ago, during my own childhood and adolescence, the mere mention of the Japanese American relocation invited controversy and vilification.

I once wrote a poem about a man who makes *shakuhachi*—the five-holed, end-blown Japanese flute made from the base of a stalk of bamboo. Its music is that of the monkish, reclusive, and meditative Buddhist tradition, and it accompanies the *shamisen* and *koto* in an ensemble music something like a classical repertoire of passionate Japanese melancholia. The maker is an amateur—he is really a dirt farmer and gardener by trade, an immigrant to this country from southern Japan who endures hardship, some real racial humiliation, and stern losses during his lifetime. He was sent, along with 120,000 other Japanese Americans to one of the relocation camps made for them during World War II after the bombing of Pearl Harbor, when the country suspected all persons of Japanese ancestry of collaboration and worse. He loses his farm, and he burns his flutes in a small fire by the bathhouse on his property, in the vain hope that eradicating all items and traces of Japanese culture will spare him from suspicion and persecution. It does not. He is sent off to the California desert—it was in the western deserts of California, Utah, Arizona, Colorado, Wyoming, and Idaho that most of these camps were built—where he is haunted by the ghosts of his old instruments that "wail like fists of wind / whistling through the barracks." He comes out of camp and rebuilds a life, becoming a more patient and less opportunistically minded man, allowing for reflection and privileging more mental acts of consolation than he had before. He becomes something of a philosopher, a poet sitting among tall canes in a bamboo grove at the edge of his property, and, near the end of his life, calling forth the music of his lost flutes to absolve him of history and its bitter losses.

It is a poem, in one version or another, that I had been trying to write since I was a child, when my maternal grandfather first told me about World War II and what it did to him and to our community. A child of nine, I thought it was a made-up story when he first told me about the camps. I asked, "How could they do this to you? And why did you go?" And then I remember talking to my parents and our neighbors and being silenced from the questioning. When I was fourteen, my grandfather told me the story again, and I went to my teachers and asked them—I was in junior high in Los Angeles—"What about this? How come we're studying World War II and you say Saipan and Okinawa, Pearl Harbor, the Battle of the Bulge, the Marshall Plan, the Berlin airlift. What about when they put 120,000 Japanese Americans into prison?—that's not in the book." My school in South Central L.A. was made up of about a thousand black students, a thousand Japanese Americans, and a thousand whites. I was marched to the back of the room and told that we would talk about this later, that I shouldn't bring it up. I asked my schoolmates in the schoolyard, "What about this?" Since I'd grown up in Hawai'i, I didn't know that you couldn't talk about it. One of the guys in my group punched me in the stomach and said, "Don't talk about it. We're not supposed to talk about it. Our parents said not to." Later on, when I was in college, I wrote a poem about this, and I showed it to my creative writing teacher—a man from a desert town in California who had gone on to Harvard for a fine education. He said, "This is a militant poem. You know, you've always been a good student. You're not here on any kind of minority admission program. You're here on academic scholarship—you don't have to be writing this sort of thing." So I took my poem back, cursing him under my breath.

About ten years later, when I was near the end of completing my first book of poems, I wanted to write about this same subject again, but in a way that wasn't like any of the ways I'd been hearing. During this time—the late seventies—there had been the Asian American movement, different kinds of student activism, and the idea emerged that we could create our own courses in Asian American Studies at places like Berkeley, UCLA, Long Beach State, and San Francisco State. But the student protest work I was seeing, the poetry from these places, was very much styled in the manner of the Last Poets, a group of urban blacks who took a revolutionary stance. Their approach was very street—bardic and insolent—characteristics I approve of socially, but somehow not in poetry. I wanted something other than that for myself, for my poetry. I wanted to write of the pain that I'd seen in the people who raised me, and their silence, their stoicism, and their reticence—in some ways their very real *dignity*.

There is a strenuous generational silence in the Japanese American community—in fact there is a two-generational silence—not only about the camps, but about an idea of an emotional life. When you have to be silent about something as cataclysmic and monumental as the relocation camps were, it tends to govern your willingness to live in *any* emotion at all. You feel your exclusion quite acutely. You feel your *difference*, your perception as an outcast *Other* in your society that is hostile to you. And you begin to internalize this hostility as self-hate—the inability to cherish your own inner life, your own social history, your own status as an individual and member of a community. At the level of the unconscious, you begin to perform an internalized silencing of your own perceptions and rewrite your story according to patterns other than those of your own life. You uphold what is *not you* and live as if your own experiences were of little value. It's kind of a censorship or handicap—an illness. And this illness lasted for two generations—the generation of the Issei, the first generation of immigrants who made a place here, and the Nisei, the second generation, native borns who grew up as teenagers during the relocation.

My generation, the third (actually I'm fourth, but in terms of age bracket I'm of the third generation), called Sansei, didn't understand this. We tried to recapture the history and talk about it, but we were angry that we were denied, not just the facts, but the emotional experience, the report, the *parenting* of knowing about our parents' and grandparents' lives. The generations before us weren't telling us their story. Without that story, we grew up cipherously—as if everything behind us was a zero and we were the first. To be without history, to be without an emotional life, to be without the ability even to *imagine* the emotional lives of the people who came before you, is an incredibly damaging thing, an ache that hurts in a way that you don't even realize hurts.

The anger we Sansei felt, and felt empowered to express, was immature of course—we simply were unable to appreciate the group stoicism in the face of the generational tragedy, to understand the curious mix of heroism and self-hate from which this stoicism emerged. Because it was for a kind of *protection* that the Nisei and Issei were so quiet. There had been so much pain, losses so incredible, that to acknowledge them might have withered hope completely, and our elders wished to spare their children this kind of despair. *Kodomo no tame* is the phrase in Japanese—sacrifice for the sake of the children—which I grew to admire as a generational code that grew out of these very real and deep feelings of shame.

When I finally understood this, after I finally became aware of and began to appreciate the very real heroism of the Nisei and Issei, I was able to write the *shakuhachi* poem from my principles as a writer—a verbal music, a simplicity and directness, the idea of cherishing the smaller things like these bamboo flutes, and an acknowledgment of history and its wanton acts. I broke through some aesthetic, political, and generational silences, and I felt like I had written something from the story of my people, telling the tale of the tribe, speaking from a mystery and a great unsaid, speaking from the ancestors and giving them a voice.

I think many tales must emerge in this way, whether they be in fiction, poetry, drama, essay, or memoir. The new ones come from something that has been held back, in a way, *prevented* by our culture, which is largely censoring and conformist, which produces a system that governs discussion—literary or otherwise—to the extent that all speech is "policed" and brought into a chain of relations dedicated to the upholding of *power* and the denigration of what is unempowered—in many cases, the stories of ethnic people, women, and other culturally underrepresented groups.

Often the telling must break through multiple layers of misunderstanding and stereotyping in order to be told. Mistellings need to be identified, confronted, and evacuated of their prestige, their cultural authority. Frank Chin has been quite righteous and entertaining in his career-long skirmish against the stereotyping of Asians in American popular culture. In "Confessions of a Number One Son," published in *Ramparts* (the forerunner to *Mother Jones*, by the way) during the early 1970s, Chin angrily and humorously confronted the issue of the Asian stereotype, ridiculing and deconstructing paternalistic American culture for its Charlie Chan, for constantly emasculating Asian men as patsies, sidekicks, eunuchs, buffoons, and maleficent villains; for exoticizing Asian women as geishas, dancing girls, courtesans, and sarong-wrapped sirens. Like Mura, he was writing against the stereotyping and silencing of Asians in our culture and made a public call for outbreaks against it.

In *The Political Unconscious*, Frederic Jameson—the foremost proponent of Frankfurt School Marxism in America—writes about how our culture gives us certain master narratives, in essence *male* narrative, which tell a story that the culture is trying to endorse. The literature, media, and even gossip conspire to give us an idea of how a life should be lived and how lives should be described in story. These stories enter our unconscious, give us our ideas of human value and human organization to the extent that we rewrite and reimagine our own experiences to conform to these master narratives. Jameson points out how these narratives flatter the political agenda of power and proliferate throughout the culture at multiple levels. We who feel woe and misery are under the domination of this kind of power.

The kind of stories promoted on television, for example— if you think of the 1950s and the Eisenhower administration and programs like the *Donna Reed Show, Ozzie and Harriet, Father Knows Best*—endorse a certain idea of family values: stability, heterosexual union, stable middle-class lifestyles, and the wisdom of the father visited upon his family—a very staid, repressive, conformist idea of life. These stories work in a way to devalue the differences and specificities in the more various kinds of lives we lead. If you happen to be Hispanic, for example, what can you find but your own self-hate after watching something like *Bachelor Father*? The ethnics are houseboys, gardeners, and the butt of jokes and recipients of the white male father's kind patronage. These kinds of things work at the level of the unconscious to the point that the individual of color, of cultural difference, feels marginalized, canceled, pushed to the edges of culture and society, feels *Othered*, feels raced, feels gendered, feels different. The story that you have from your own life, then, is thus canceled, and you have begun to hate it, you have begun to live in a silence that's unarticulated by our culture. This is part of what Jameson means about the nature of the political unconscious—it creates revolutionary alienation.

At the same time, Jameson suggests that the new stories are going to be coming from those who feel silence, who feel othered, whose stories are not taken up by culture and society and proliferated throughout the system; that the new narrative will reorder experience in a completely unexpected way. In this context, I'm reminded of a book by Tillie Olsen called *Silences*, which is mostly about women and women's lives, and how they are not portrayed by our master literature as revealed by the higher preponderance of male writers in the *Norton Anthology of English Literature*. As a child of the Asian diaspora, I felt that the master narratives of America were not open to me either, would not easily incorporate stories that I knew except as addenda to the grander tales of Manifest Destiny, white settlement of the West, and the idea of "civilization" being brought to Hawai'i by Christian missionaries and planters. For most of my adolescence and early adult life, I felt that there was no literary matrix in which I could address the histories of the immigration and plantation experience in Hawai'i, and my own stories went completely untold. But, slowly at first, I began to reexamine some of my misguided values about the folktales I grew up with—Jataka tales of the Buddha, supernatural tales set in Hawai'i, Japanese folktales, oral histories of immigrants and laborers on the Hawaiian sugar plantations—and I realized that, because of my education and my partaking of the values of the mainstream culture, I'd seriously repressed my own cognizance of these tales to the point that I'd engaged in the process of denying, even to myself, that these were worthy tales of human wisdom. I'd become *colonized*, and I needed to begin the process of mental *de-colonization*. I needed to acknowledge the specificities of Japanese American history, and I needed to recognize that there was great value in the oral histories and Asian folktales and even in the structure of those tales. I needed to reverse the process of cultural self-hate. And it was that process that brought me into writing a poem like "Something Whispered in the *Shakuhachi*" and an essay like "Kubota," included in this collection, which partake of the traumatic history of the Japanese American relocation and try to give homage to the emotional lives of the generations before mine.

It would be marvelous if the normal response to this kind of outbreak against a culturally imposed silence were one of welcome and the acknowledgment of a fresh and contributive perspective but this is not always the case. Quite often, the response can be social hostility, misunderstanding, and severe personal punishment visited upon the writer who has broken the silence. Once an initial breakthrough is accomplished, that is, once the censoring powers of the political unconscious of centralized culture are somehow thrown off or defeated, silence, as a cultural code, still carries within its operations a note of the sacred that undergirds and perpetuates its maintenance. Power constantly maintains itself and polices those under its domination. And power is insidious—it often masquerades as resistance to power, inverting principles, exchanging roles, proliferating in a cultural hall of mirrors that distort, multiply, and disguise its operations. Therefore, a secondary breakthrough still has to be made—this time one that is against the censoring powers of the *margin* rather than those of the center. If the cultural war is successfully fought on the first front and the censoring mechanisms of the mainstream culture are overcome, then there is yet another cultural front, equally powerful, that arises and must be engaged. The literary speaker against silence can still be severely punished, this time by the ethnic Other rather than by centralized cultural power. The Asian American writer can be victimized by those who have themselves been silenced, by voices purporting to emerge from within ethnic communities, making exclusive claims to political truth and raising challenges against a given writer's ethnic authenticity. What follows are a few examples of what I think are instances of "internalized oppression"— manifestations of social oppression and exercises of hierarchical political power that sometimes emerge from *within* the enclave cultures of peoples of color.

Back in 1971, the Asian American Studies Center at UCLA published *Roots*, the first Asian American reader. *Roots* contained academic papers, political essays, memoir, poetry, photography, and graphic arts; and there was also an extended piece of literary criticism in it. Written from a Marxist perspective by graduate student Bruce Iwasaki and given the carefully worded title "Response and Change for the Asian in America: A Survey of Asian American Literature," the article surveys the history of Asian American literature up until that point and makes some provocative judgments regarding two pioneering Asian American writers—Frank Chin and Lawson Fusao Inada. In essence, Iwasaki criticizes them for being more interested in their own sensibilities and in the problem of developing an authentic Asian American literary diction than in the "welfare of the Asian American community" as a whole. Iwasaki accuses Chin and Inada of using the Asian American community primarily to give "local color" to their works, ignoring that their "artistic decisions are tied with moral and . . . political decisions." As a final pronouncement, Iwasaki writes the "Chin and Inada remain within the bounds that makes so much literature *safe.*"

I was inspired by what Chin and Inada were writing then, so Iwasaki's complaints surprised, perplexed, and even angered me. He seemed to be chastising writers for not promoting his own concept of community needs, his own political and academic agendas. Chin and Inada, if nothing else, seem to me always to be about doing what they want as writers—like Whitman, they are the perennial unwashed ruffians of culture. Which, I assume, was what bothered Iwasaki. He could not annex their work to his own ends, he could not dictate theme, tone, or agenda to them. Like Matthew Arnold and Plato, he elevates the critical mind over the creative, has a vested interest in engineering culture and society, and therefore had great difficulty tolerating the aesthetic independence and unpredictability of writers like Chin and Inada, who seemed to me heroic for that reason.

During the summer of 1989, on a book tour after the publication of her novel *The Floating World*, writer Cynthia Kadohata, a Japanese American, was making a routine appearance at Cody's Books in Berkeley. The crowd was unusually large for a first-time novelist, packed with interested Asian American students and some UC faculty too. Her book had been receiving good notices in the mainstream press, and a chapter of it had run in the *New Yorker* prior to publication. She read quietly but clearly, with a fine delicacy of voice and a minimum of physical movement. The audience seemed charmed. But, during the question and answer session that followed, she was chastised for not writing about the concentration camp experience. Her novel, partially set during the time of World War II, tells the story of an itinerant family of Japanese Americans wandering through the West and South in search of work, doing without community except for each other. It never once mentions the federally ordered evacuation of citizens of Japanese ancestry from the West Coast. But there was a powerful faction among Japanese American intellectuals who felt it was illegitimate of Kadohata to have refrained from any overt references to the internment camp experience.

"You mean to tell me that you have this family of Japanese Americans running around through Arizona, Colorado, and Utah, and you *never* say anything about the camps!" a scholar shouted from the audience. "You should be ashamed of yourself for falsifying our history!" he yelled.

More shouting ensued as a few other Asian Americans joined this public castigation. Kadohata responded by saying that she didn't *intend* to write about the camps, that her novel wasn't *about* the camps, that she was writing about a family of loners and misfits, writing from *her* experience, and that was that. She was then criticized for abdicating her responsibilities as a Japanese American writer, denounced for not fulfilling expectation, for not writing from the public truth of the time.

She told me later that the whole incident puzzled and upset her. It hurt that people, especially other Asian Americans, felt compelled to attack her for what she *didn't* write even more than for what she *did* write. Kadohata was wondering why there was so much vehemence, so much anger, and so much "attitude" among Asian American writers. She hadn't defended herself then, but the episode made a deep and lasting impression. She told me that the next time she was out there, she'd be ready. She wasn't going to get beaten up again without a fight.

I once remarked that Asian America is so immature as a culture and so unused to seeing cultural representations of itself that, whenever representation does occur, many respond with anger because of the pain released. It is as if they recognize *their* story in the outlines of the story one of the writers is telling, but feel even more alienated rather than absolved because that story isn't theirs *exactly*, or doesn't present the precise tone and tenor of their inner feeling regarding an experience they feel the writer, as an Asian American, should understand. It's like a bunch of family members at a holiday dinner sitting around, trying to tell a story about a maiden aunt, a matriarch, or a black sheep. One starts it up, and before you know it, six others chime in, saying the first didn't get it right, that their version is the one that is true and has all the facts. It has to do with issues of primacy, proprietorship, a claim of proper descent and legitimacy, and a claim to specialized knowledge. It is complex. And charged with passion. Whenever someone singles out a certain storyline, and interpretive angle, there are always those who would dispute its legitimacy, even to the point of trying to erode the confidence of the storyteller.

During the summer of 1990, I was in Volcano, Hawai'i, making trips through the rain forest there, taking field notes for my book about the place. I was home sorting through files when the telephone rang. It was a woman who told me she was the West Coast reporter for the *Philadelphia Inquirer*, asking my opinion of Maxine Hong Kingston's literary contributions, asking whether or not she influenced my own work in any way. I said, "If it weren't for Maxine Hong Kingston, I wouldn't have my imaginative life. It was a great moment reading *China Men*. That book released human feeling for me. It humanized me, it released my own stories for me." I said that *China Men* gave me the inspiration to envision the lives of my own ancestors, particularly the men in my family, in a way that I had been blocked from doing. Her work was liberating, I felt, and it gave me my own grandfathers back.

Time passed, and I heard nothing about the piece. Then, about a year later, I started getting letters and postcards from writers, white and Asian, all around the country, mentioning some newspaper flap between Frank Chin, our pioneering editor of Asian American writing, and Maxine Hong Kingston, perhaps the most eminent Asian American writer. Friends in Honolulu phoned and mentioned it too. Some congratulated me for my "brave remarks." All wanted to know what I thought about the supposed debate. But I thought nothing, not knowing what everyone was referring to. I tried to ignore the whole thing.

But then a postcard came from Maxine Hong Kingston herself. It said something like this: "Thank you for your kind remarks about my work. It was the first time any Asian American male writer has said anything in print that was *positive* about my writing."

I was astonished and a little embarrassed. "How could *that* be?" I asked myself. How could an omission like that be possible? Her books had been around for about fifteen years by then. And everyone knows their huge impact. But there was that strange phrase in her note—"Asian American *male* writer." Why was *gender* important here? What could she be talking about?

I called James Houston, a novelist who is a mutual friend, in Santa Cruz. Houston is coauthor with his wife, Jeanne Wakatsuki Houston, of *Farewell to Manzanar*, the first book to treat the Japanese American relocation camp experience that gained popular acceptance. I thought he might be able to illuminate things for me, being on the Mainland and probably "in the loop" for this kind of writerly controversy. He told me that various articles had come out in the *Los Angeles Times, San Jose Mercury News*, and *San Francisco Chronicle* putting forward the story that there was a gender split between Asian American male writers and Asian American female writers. They put Frank Chin at the center of the argument, along with Maxine Hong Kingston and Amy Tan. They quoted Chin as saying the Kingston and Tan had won wide audience appeal because they pandered to white tastes and promulgated a stereotypical exotic image, particularly of Asian women. Chin used words like "traitors," "feminist assimilators," and "whores" when talking about Kingston and Tan, describing their work as "white racist art," then raging on about how Kingston, in particular, gets Chinese myth, language, and culture completely wrong. The articles collected opinions about the controversy from various other Asian Americans, me included, and the comments fell pretty much on both sides of the issue. Houston said that my remarks were some of the strongest, and he read me more of what I was quoted as saying.

"People are approaching ethnicity with a religious fundamentalism," I said in the *San Jose Mercury News*. "They want to discredit and repress certain works from the canon of Asian American writing. They want to be the arbiters of what constitutes worth in Asian American literature. The problem is they're trying to exert control over all the rest of us." Along with playwright David Henry Hwang and critic Elaine Kim, I came off defending the phenomenon of Kingston's and Tan's popularity.

This was my introduction to the social force that rocked throughout the Asian American writerly community for the next couple of years. Wherever I went, whether it was UC Berkeley or Williams College in Massachusetts, whether it was the Asia Society in New York or the Asian American Studies Center at UCLA, students wanted to know where I stood on the issue. Every Asian American literary event I was a part of took up the controversy as a central theme. Academics started framing scholarly presentations accordingly, devoting whole panels at the Asian American Studies Convention to the examination and discussion of the issues of the gender split and the debate between Chin and Kingston. The purported split was tone-setting and divisive.

White academics had identified a gender war in mainstream writing, African Americans had identified one in black writing, and, it seemed, Asian Americans had the mimetic desire to define one among our own writers. Thereafter, discussion of our literature constantly proceeded from the assumption of division and divisiveness among the writers, based either on a gender split or another, even more pernicious dichotomy. Asian American students I met, either in large groups or individually, began to take it as article of faith that there were "radical" and "authentic" Asian American writers, and contrasted these with those who were "sellout" and "inauthentic" writers. Chin and other somewhat underpublished writers would be in the "authentic" camp, while Tan and Kingston led the "inauthentic" camp. As I wrote in the introduction to *The Open Boat: Poems from Asian America*, this kind of thinking led to the creation of a litmus test of ethnic authenticity. If a writer was adjudged successful in the larger culture, either by best-seller popularity or by virtue of certain awards, then this very success invalidated that writer as an *authentic* Asian American one. This judgment often licensed out-and-out rudeness toward some Asian American writers when they visited college and university campuses. Others could be excluded for "inauthenticity" or boycotted by the faithful if their visits arose from an invitation by an English Department rather than from Ethnic Studies.

Such divisions serve as a kind of *policing* mechanism of the ethnic culture, governing the range of allowable literary production. At the level of the unconscious, then, the level of unspoken agreement, to be an "Asian American writer" meant subscription to a code of cultural and political values that excluded certain mainstream literary practices—perhaps rhetorical eloquence, perhaps Anglophone tradition-based style and structure in poetry, perhaps mass-market success in fiction, perhaps subjective personal accounts as opposed to jargonized sociological treatises in nonfiction. Chin's criticism of Tan and Kingston and the subsequent public brouhaha had set up a kind of operating cultural myth that divided the small community of Asian American writers into easily distinguishable and, to my mind, grossly oversimplified binary opposites. This myth of opposition, unfortunately, was then readily taken up by the Asian American community of students and academics.

I'd witnessed this phenomenon before. I was a first-year graduate student at the University of Michigan in 1975 when a group of us raised some student funds to invite Native American novelist Leslie Marmon Silko, African American poet Etheridge Knight, and Japanese American poet Lawson Fusao Inada to read on campus. We got monies from a coalition of minority student groups, and we arranged for the black fraternity on campus to host the event. The poet Robert Hayden, author of

"The Middle Passage," an epic poem about the slave trade, was a professor on the English faculty there at the time. Fiftyish, past six feet and large-framed, he wore thick, Coke-bottle glasses and always had a greeting for me whenever our paths crossed, usually in the poetry room of the English building. There weren't very many people of color around the poetry world at Michigan at the time, and Hayden was a hero of mine, a quiet man who wrote delicate, sometimes mournful lyrics about his childhood in Detroit. He came from the same neighborhood as the boxer Joe Louis. He'd taught at Fisk University, an exclusively black institution in Nashville, Tennessee, and he had lived a while enduring enforced segregation and de facto Jim Crow segregation. I looked up to him, and I invited him to join the group at the podium.

His answer surprised me. "While I want to honor your folks," Hayden said, "and while it flatters me to be asked, I'm afraid that I must decline your invitation, Garrett."

I was astonished. When I asked him why, he said, "Did you ever hear of the term 'Uncle Tom,' son?"

I nodded, shocked it could apply to him.

"Well," Hayden said, "I'm afraid the black students around here think of me as just another Uncle Tom—a corny, submissive Negro shuffling around the white folks. I am *obsolete*. And I am afraid that I am *persona non grata* around African American Studies. I think it would hurt your cause if I appeared on the podium with the other writers. Students might boycott, and that wouldn't help you build the kind of feeling or audience I think you want."

I held him in conversation for a little while longer. I may have asked him why the black students thought of him that way, but he didn't have to answer. I knew about the attitude. Hayden was professorial, learned, mild in his social personality. The model in play for the black poet then was what came out of Black Power and the Black Arts movement. It was a brilliant, pissed-off male in a black leather jacket, wearing a Che beret and sermonizing about the revolution. I had heard Black Panther David Hilliard speak. I had heard black revolutionary poets Stanley Crouch, Quincy Troupe, and Ojinke read at the Watts Writers' Workshop. I had heard Amiri Baraka give a speech to black students at Michigan in 1974, excoriating them, sermonizing and hectoring them. It was an exhilarating performance. What ran as universal among all of these presentations was a stance that had emerged out of black patriarchy and black urban experience. It was Stagolee—the legendary black gambler who could get away with murder if he wanted to. It was black male defiance in proud opposition to dominant white society. And Robert Hayden did not fit that model at all.

Don't get me wrong. I *liked* the revolutionary stance. It was entertaining and empowering and, as a young Asian American male, I needed both. But I also admired Hayden and cherished the tenderness of his verses. I was troubled that the revolution could not move aside to make a space for him and his work as well, that learning, gentleness, and a soft social manner would be so rejected and condemned. In contemporary terms, I understood that Hayden was adjudged or, at the very least, suspected as being "white identified," and therefore ostracized from the mainstream of black student and literary life. As a poet and mentor for blacks, he was looked upon as a kind of oxbow lake in a meandering river of cultural evolution. And I was sorry about that.

Our multiethnic coalition went on with the event, which was a huge success, and Robert Hayden came, though he did not speak from the podium. A ripple went through the crowd, a mix of Third World students, as we called ourselves then, when he entered the room with his wife, people moving aside as his large frame lumbered through the aisles and down to the front row center seats I'd reserved for him. I remember that Lawson Inada and Etheridge Knight both acknowledged him from the podium. Hayden meant something to them too. And the man did not speak a word to our audience that night. Among we students at the University of Michigan, Robert Hayden had been silenced.

For this anthology, I tried to choose essays written *against* social silencing, but emerging from deep personal silences dedicated to reflecting upon moral, political, and identity issues. They are written *against* cultural conformism, intransigent rationalisms, and convenient pragmatisms all vying for space in the mind, all making exclusive claims regarding the truths of our experiences. Their progress is toward a different kind of resolution than that made available by most other mechanisms of society—be they systems of justice, social welfare, or community organization. One of the central things these essays *are* about, it seems to me, is an *arrest* of the practical mind so that the mind of memory and imagination can then be engaged, calling forth the purpose of taking pure pleasure in the meditative act of writing itself. This is the exercise of symbolic imagination to no purpose but the achievement of a kind of resolution known as aesthetic composure or, to be sublime, rapture. One of the things writers try to achieve, perhaps even more than any kind of moral decision or political vision, is the moment of literary *pleasure*, a feeling that does not depend on any other logic except that dictated by the world of its own language, its recollections and interpretations of events, its need for or dismissal of practical resolutions to its inner problematics. To risk an even more venturesome statement, I would say that these essays are *written against power* to achieve a consistency of their own fictions—an otherworldly power of their own—so that the writing itself can stand separate from any sacerdotal class of interpreters (academics, intellectuals, political organizers) and undermine the ruling doxologies, be they of race or class or ethnic group, whatever ideology would claim itself to be the norm of thinking.

To varying degrees, I think important cultural stories that need to be told generally go this way. They emerge from long-held silences, and, with most cases, the storyteller has had to have spent a good deal of time mulling over the issues before breaking that silence. Sometimes the stories are received with welcome, but, too often, the stories meet with strenuous resistance, and the culture restricts their proliferation and tries to negate their authority. The writers whose essays I chose for *Under Western Eyes: Personal Essays from Asia America* each speak from this kind of acute silencing. They are trying to expose issues, authorize suppressed histories, and articulate experiences that, in general, have *not* been spoken to before. Many included here quest for stories of immigration and the hardships of acculturation, stories that have been silenced somehow, pushed to the margins by an idea of common culture, a homogeneity of belief in certain kinds of social and even spiritual values that push aside not only the new tales, but, in fact, even our means of perceiving and recognizing our individual experiences. The operating notion that there is such a thing as a common or universal culture, in effect, pushes aside very specific experiences that don't happen to flatter what is assumed to be the common agenda of the country. This notion devalues stories about women, for example, stories about people of color, stories of gender, stories that are somehow forbidden and tagged as aberrational, as militant, as depraved. This is the kind of silencing I'm talking about too—the kind of silencing felt by the Japanese Americans about the relocation. The kind of silencing that was enforced even *within* the Japanese American community.

For a writer, as you live in this kind of silence, in this kind of misery, not knowing quite what it is that the world is not giving you, not knowing quite what it is that your work cannot address as yet, you are at the beginning of a critique of culture and society. It is the moment when powerful personal alienation slips into critical thinking—the origin of imagination. It is this initial step of intellection that enables the emergence of new, transformative, even revolutionary creativity. It occurs at the juncture between the production of art and the exercise of deep critical thought.

It is in this way that the new stories emerge from the shadows and margins of cultural disapproval and come into a piece of writing. The personal essay and memoir, in particular, seem well suited as literary vehicles for this kind of self-examination and historically recuperative storytelling. The personal history and the "ethnic" story, the giving of testimony, the journeys of consciousness, and the providing of witness to the operations of racism in our society—these come together in a piece of writing to create a complex literary substitute for the unconscious matrixes of cultural legitimacy and social understanding that exist for others who see themselves as more "central." Citizens comfortable organizing or deriving their personal identities under the codes of cultural centrality don't feel quite as strong a need to have an ethnic or racial history explained for them—theirs exist in the standard textbooks, in the movies, in TV commercials and prime-time programs. But those citizens who emerge from marginalized histories, from complicated and fractured loyalties, need a means to probe the inner life, the ideological conflicts, and the repressed communal histories in order to create identity.

In "The Faintest Echo of Our Language," Chang-rae Lee illustrates his intense love and gratitude for, even loyalty to, the music and beauty in the Korean language his mother was hearing at the moment of her death. In "Mother Tongue," Amy Tan writes about how she took courage and inspiration from the way her mother spoke English, mixing it into Chinese syntax, transcending and beautifying its Anglophone roots. They sway our linguistic orientations and expectations, and honor the mixing of languages in our American culture; and, in the process, they honor the Asian diaspora and the mother tongue of our America. They search for a new way to see the spoken languages in our lives, how they bear remnants of culture and promises of great emotion, how in speaking them, we writers express our need to seek new poles of narrative and cultural orientation rather than those more readily available, even in books.

I think each of the writers in *Under Western Eyes* has gone through a decolonization process, rejecting the master cultural narratives and, in their place, insisting on the new stories emerging from silence. "Silence and the Graverobbers" by Lillian Ho Wan and "Bad Blood" by Geraldine Kudaka assemble the fragments of suppressed and underimagined familial and cultural histories. They talk about stereotyping, prohibitions of identity, and the tyranny of social expectations based on race and gender. Memoirs like David Low's "Winterblossom Garden," a poignant tale of the struggles of his immigrant parents, and John Yau's "A Little Memento from the Boys," a fulminant and streetwise fable, are narratives that give testimony to the process of urban acculturation and cultural resistance among Chinese Americans. Peter Bacho does something similar regarding Filipino Americans in "The Second Room," yet he also explodes the stereotype regarding one of the greatest macho myths of our culture. Bacho was a student of Bruce Lee's principal disciple in a kung-fu school in Seattle, and his memoir gives dimension and personal poignancy to the adolescent quest narrative in place in our culture regarding the martial arts.

156

The personal essay, as a literary form, seems to lend itself quite easily to the kind of internal questing with which so many here have been engaged. Like the lyric poem, the personal essay is an intensely subjective genre, insisting on individual sensibility and consciousness as the final court of arbitration for issues somehow undealt with by society. It places the individual, its author and hero, at some contemplative remove from dailiness, providing a kind of "momentary stay against confusion" so that a certain obsession can be indulged, a troubling question can be wrestled with, an evanescent experience, as yet unchronicled by the culture, can be recorded. Yet, unlike the shorter lyric, the personal essay gives itself over to copiousness and development, incorporating anecdote, personal history, rumination, and discursiveness and allowing for extended reflection upon events that would have to be compressed or metaphorized in poetry, or made somehow less intimate and questioning in a fictional narrative. The development of a self becomes one of the stories embedded within the personal essay, and, in the selections collected here, the story of that development is one of Asian Americans arriving at a consciousness evolved within the fractures of available identities and elective affinities, whether literary or popular. It involves the *imperative* of having been *raced* by this culture, of the individual having no account for the social and cultural forces that threaten to marginalize or suppress both individual experience and the potential for collective identification with Asians in America. These narratives involve questions of race, ethnic history, and the interpersonal set against a backdrop of education and society resistant to the development of individual and ethnic identities.

It is interesting to note that many of the contributions here were written by poets. Li-Young Lee, a poet with two well-known books, contributes a fond and pained remembrance of his magisterial father who was a Presbyterian cleric for a poor parish in Pennsylvania, but who was also, prior to immigrating to America, the personal physician to Mao Tse-tung and a perennial refugee. Lee's memoir reports on a complicated history and on the development of an even more complicated aesthetic and moral consciousness. In "The Internment of Desire," Sansei poet David Mura tells the story of the development of his own sexual consciousness—a subject that has largely been silenced concerning Asian Americans, particularly males. His essay is frank and confessional, and it addresses the hidden relationship between the pattern of development of carnal desire and that of ethnic and personal consciousness. "Lalita Mashe" is Chitra Divakaruni's tragic portrait of a "No-Name Woman" back in her native India, a story of victimization that would be forgotten were it not for the obsessive loyalties of one who lives with a consciousness of diaspora—Divakaruni, standing on a BART platform in Oakland, sights the ghost of the dead woman going the other way on a train, and it is the incongruity that triggers her memory and imagination. As with so much poetry, it is a powerful and unforgettable image that compels the rest of the writing, the unfolding of the story behind the mysterious and symbolic image. Perhaps, feeling the lack of the kind of historical, emotional, and intellectual foregrounding provided for poets who identify with central culture, these Asian American poets have gravitated to the memoir and personal essay to fill this psychological absence. They must "explain" themselves beyond what is possible in a lyric.

Indeed, it is the job of an essayist to explain, and so we have story, history, recollection, and rumination bundled into one extended yet highly poetic piece of writing by Jeanne Wakatsuki Houston. Her "Colors" is a kind of compressed epic, an "explanation of a life." NPR reporter Nguyen Qui-Duc's "A Taste of Home" is a heartbreaking report on his return to Saigon years after having fled it. He struggles with feeling privileged and saved as he compares himself, in terms of body and mind, to those who stayed behind in Ho Chi Minh City. Nguyen's portrait of an elementary school classmate he encounters on the street is tinged with pity and regret even as his catalogue of the physical surroundings and his profile of the typical, quite alcoholic life led by so many contemporary Vietnamese male laborers are somewhat hard-boiled.

"Telling Differences" by Debra Kang Dean and "Where Are You From?" by Geeta Kothari address the powerful inner conflict and soul-searching that go on when one becomes aware of the subtle racism beneath the surface of so much of daily interaction. In seemingly innocuous events like Kothari's shopping for a dress in a trendy boutique and Dean's work as a student editor on a university magazine, the effects of racism within our culture conspire to repress their self-esteem as people of color. In Kothari's case, it is that constant feeling of being cast as an outsider, being automatically denied her status as an acculturated American because of her skin color. Dean can't abide the racist notions implicit in a poem being considered by the editor of the magazine she works for, and resigns in protest, which triggers a complicated sequence of events of social pressuring—her fellow student editors argue with her, try to persuade her against her own instincts, challenge the legitimacy of her protest, diminish the seriousness of the matter, and ostracize her for betraying the belief system of the social group to which she had once belonged. She talks about social trauma versus individual awareness, mutuality versus consciousness, and she chooses the path consciousness demands. Her essay chronicles the interior process of creating a complex social analysis with high personal stakes. Both Kothari and Dean struggle against the social silencing that tries to deny the legitimacy of their own interpretation of events. These writings are heroic in that they not only oppose the powerful pressures to uphold the legitimacy of mainstream values, even in its interpretation of events, but in that they also identify and carefully delineate what would otherwise be invisible pressures. They expose the operations of silencing.

A couple of years ago, I got a phone call at my home in Oregon from a reporter at *Newsday*, the daily paper for Long Island. Just the day before, Robert Olen Butler had been awarded the Pulitzer Prize for his collection of short stories called *A Good Scent from a Strange Mountain*. The narrator of each story is Vietnamese, each a different survivor of the war in Vietnam, most of them living in this country. The reporter wanted to know what I, as an Asian American writer, thought about the prize being awarded to a white male who wrote stories in the personae of male and female Vietnamese refugees.

I told him I was personally delighted that Butler had won the Pulitzer, that I was glad that the prize had finally gone to someone who was known as a dedicated laborer in the fields of creative writing, who wrote for long years in obscurity, who wrote well and without recognition except from his peers in the business, who taught a heavy teaching load at a regional branch of a state university, who was a single parent who gave to his community and to the community of Vietnamese immigrants. I stalled, wanting a little time to think.

"Yes," the reporter said, "but what is your opinion about his being white and writing in the voices of Asians? Of him *adopting* the identity of Vietnamese individuals in order to write his fiction?"

I had suspected there was something hot behind his questioning. On matters of race, American culture has the chronic habit of organizing itself in terms of opposition first, even with regard to a book that, to me, was a sincere attempt to create commonality.

On the one hand, there was my own feeling that Butler's book was kind of a breakthrough for American books on the Vietnam experience. Until Butler published his stories, most every piece of writing from Americans had to do with the tragedy of the American experience in Vietnam. Tim O'Brien and Larry Heinemann had written powerful fiction from the point of view of American soldiers. Michael Herr had published nonfiction from a similar perspective, while Yusef Komunyakaa had written a stunning book of poems—it, too, based on his GI experience. Very little had been published from the Vietnamese point of view, and almost nothing about the Vietnamese experience in America. Butler's book had created characters and described an ethos much unknown to mainstream American—that of the Viet Kieu, Vietnamese survivors of the war who had emigrated to the United States and were struggling over their losses, their identity, and the difficulties of acculturation. Sympathetic without being sentimental, Butler's treatment gave the outlines of their lives great human dimension and humor without ignoring the multiple tragedies of their having lost homelands, loved ones, and a certain continuity of cultural identity. *A Good Scent from a Strange Mountain*, though written by someone who was white and not Vietnamese, could not easily be seen as yet another piece of "minstrelsy" by the white culture ventriloquizing the ethnic experience and colonizing the mind of the Other for the purpose of reinforcing cultural dominance. It is a work that seemed to me at once more complex than that, and yet I could not say so within the simplistic framework in which the reporter was asking his question.

I told the reporter that I couldn't give him a short answer and gave him the long one instead. I begged off making any kind of *ultimate* political judgment. Since I am not from the Vietnamese American community, I couldn't presume to speak to the issue of whether or not his characterizations and tales infringed upon some "right" of theirs to define themselves in our culture. I felt uncomfortable being asked to speak "as an Asian American," knowing that we are an extremely diverse group in terms of generations, cultures of origin, and economics. I urged him to ask a Vietnamese American. I told him that, by asking me for my opinion, I knew he was operating as if Asians in America were one vast, homogeneous category, and making the false assumption that any one of us, no matter that our ethnicities were different, could speak "on behalf" of the entire race.

He tried to press me, but gave up after a few more exchanges. He couldn't pin me down because I didn't want to be. Frustrated, the reporter thanked me and hung up. It was obvious I hadn't helped his story angle. He wanted a fight between Butler and Asians, and he wanted me either to defend Butler or to attack him. He wanted my answers to be *simple* and unqualified. On one side or the other. I guess, on that issue, I was sitting on a fence. The reporter's coming to me was itself another act of racism, and I worried about participating in that.

But I continued to feel uncomfortable about the incident. Why couldn't I have given the reporter something more definitive? Why hadn't I been more ready to give a strong opinion on the matter? What was it that made me speak on both sides of the issue? Was I, in fact, in being so equivocal, acting as an apologist for white colonization of ethnic cultural space? Was I—of *all* things—acting like a goddamn Uncle Tom? What are the issues here and how could I rethink myself through them? I questioned myself but hesitated to bring it up among my friends, whether Asian or not. I feared policing and I feared judgment. I wanted some space to think. I decided to look for other writers who could help me to do this kind of thinking.

There was indeed a political dimension to this issue, but it is not one regarding a given writer's "right" to represent a culture.

There is a profound difference between the idea that any group has an exclusive right to engage in authorized acts of cultural representation and the idea that cultural representations are not open to criticism, whether by a group or an individual critic. Although our system of prestige can itself be seen as a kind of rule of unwritten laws, I believe that we cannot, finally, create legislation regarding cultural properties in the verbal arts—that is, provide cultural laws empowering and licensing only certain individuals to do what we will prohibit others from doing with regard to language and the arts. At the same time, I do not think that anyone can be above being criticized for what they choose to do with this kind of liberty. I think we can applaud Mura for raising a political objection to a work of art, but we can also critique—though not silence—Butler on political grounds for the work of art he has produced. I think we can critique Mura as well, and we can praise Butler too—for his humanistic politics as well as for his powerful artistry. The confusions, then, have less to do with the practices of the individual artists and much more to do with the way general thought in our culture (as enacted by media and the ephemeral communal mind) tends to oversimplify complex social and artistic issues, with the habitual comminglings and false oppositions of matters of art with matters of social justice. The problem, ultimately, has to do with confusing and, finally, conflating the two realms.

I think David Mura was coming from a mainly *political* critique of *Miss Saigon* when he protested the casting policies of its producer. Empowered by his own rising ethnic consciousness and a fresh understanding of the operations of the racial stereotypes in our culture, he raised political and social objections to an instance of racism. That he protested its manifestation in a work of popular art was an attempt at critique of the *system* and not of the artists—not of the playwright, not of the actor. The casting of a white actor as Eurasian was an infringement upon Asian identity enacted systemically, through the coalescence of power assembled in the lack of political awareness in the play's producer coupled with the tacit, unconscious approval of the larger portion of American society culturally comfortable with the notion of a white playing a person of color. Yet, Mura did not ask that a writer be silenced or that political controversy dictate the cancellation of the play. He made a critique, a fairly modest, if socially powerful, literary objection. Mura was an individual expressing conscientious objection to a systemic cultural problem. He politicized an instance of unconsciously created racism manifested in a work of popular art. His protest occurred at the very line of collision between art and politics, but I do not believe he confused one with the other, nor did he mistake what the relationship was between a single writer and systemic power.

Yet, our culture often does. In contrast to Mura's objection to the casting of *Miss Saigon*, the political issue that the *Newsday* reporter raised around Robert Olen Butler's book of stories proceeds from the notion that an individual writer could be *silenced* or censured as somehow not representative of an ethnic group or improperly representative of an ethnic group. Behind this is the further notion that a given group could claim exclusive proprietary rights to all representations of itself created in the culture. A notion like this would establish that ethnic topics, ethnic identities, and the literary portrayal of ethnic voices were the *exclusive cultural properties* of a group that would somehow be deemed "authentic," licensed with the cultural "right" to represent itself as the ethnic *Other*.

Setting aside the enormously complex problem of identifying exactly *who* would constitute this authentic group and exactly *how* ethnicity is to be identified, it would still remain that this ethnic group would possess the right to silence any individual it deemed "inauthentic" or otherwise undesirable. This would grant the identified group the power of high censorship over the individual writer, thus creating yet another system of cultural silencing and, in microcosm of and mirroring the mainstream, reproducing the tyrannical situation of group dominance over the individual artist. It is yet another form of cultural centrality that would itself create margins within a cultural margin, that would reproduce cultural hierarchies and replicate, within ethnic enclaves, mainstream-like relationships of repressive group power over individual expression. It is system against individual and yet another manifestation of the conservative workings of the political unconscious.

The other instances I cite are acts of severe silencing that were attempts to create fear and acrimony around literary production itself, victimizing isolable writers with a damaged climate around the social reception of their work. Such efforts are attempts to capture, manage, and assemble social power and bring it to bear in censure upon an individual. This is a powerful, inevitably volatile encounter that encroachers upon artistic freedoms, asking art to play out politics and conscripting the artist to be an ally in the war to achieve a perfect social justice. When the artist refuses the conscription or is perceived to have refused, or when the artist performs in a manner that is perceived as inimical to the political agendas of an ethnic group to which that writer is perceived to belong, then critique of the writer can sometimes escalate into social and political censure. This is when the principles of artistic freedom become compromised. Mainstream fears of ethnic individuation and an ethnic group's agitprop suppression of an individual's consciousness emerge from such motives. The possessiveness felt by an ethnic group for cultural representations of its history too frequently results in authorizing unfortunate acts of literary tyranny. Those who see art primarily as an instrument of social engineering are allied, at an extreme, with thinkers like Joseph Stalin and Jesse Helms.

I myself think it's time to break away from debates couched in terms of opposition that ask artists of color to make oversimplified choices between politics and art. We cannot adjudicate justice in society by infringing upon the freedom of our artists. To oppose social responsibility to artistic freedom is itself a crime. The realm of art, what sixth-century Han Chinese called "the water margin," is where the dispossessed go when they have lost the possibility of getting justice in society. I believe one powerful justification for artistic freedom is that human judgment itself is first cultivated and refined in acts of imagination, and then applied to political and social practices. Wrongdoing cannot be made right until recognized as wrongdoing, until it is *perceived* as such. And the artist (along with those in the media) is at least one of those citizens who can both create and change our perceptions.

The writers included in *Under Western Eyes* have been engaged in the project of trying to free these political, artistic, and personal issues from each other, carefully mulling over problems of consciousness, characterization, and political infringement not only of any given group but of any given individual, including the writers themselves. As subjective personal accounts and *not* pieces of cultural legislation (not even artistic decrees or manifestos), the essays included here are poised at the point of collision between notions of culture and the personal, and they try to negotiate the tricky mental ground between the twin imperatives toward the creation of an affecting human portraiture and the social wishes for the fulfillment of a necessary justice. Their enterprises have to do with finding the fine psychic strands of human intuition as they respond to the wanton acts of history and, based on the ensuing discoveries, writing new histories.

I think acts of imagination are precisely what *enable* just politics. As written acts loyal to extremely specific *ethoi* and eschewing reliance upon the complex of notions regarding central values and shared histories that would otherwise be known as *natural* (or, worse yet, as *universal*), these essays have struck out into fresh territories of consciousness and ethnic histories in order to establish a new relationship with cultural power. Though art cannot itself bring justice about, yet it calls for justice to be done. Literature itself is always an outbreak of some kind, a turning away from social pressures and issues so that the writer can mull things over in a meditational space that might reorganize not only the issues, but, potentially speaking, society itself. In this sense, these essays are *foundational*, more primary perhaps than fiction, epic in intent if not scope. They are about the making of new Americans.

Volcano, Hawai'i

Gardens We Have Left

When I was six, my family was living in Kahuku, Hawai'i, on the windward north shore of the island of O'ahu, a place since 1888 that was dedicated, until twenty years ago, to the cultivation of sugar cane. The abandoned cane fields still dominate the strip of flat land between the ocean and the green cliffs of the Ko'olau Mountains, remnants of one of the volcanoes that built the island. As you go east, driving the highway there, a blue sea will be to your left while the green sea of pitching cane will be to your right. As a child, I saw workers flailing machetes in the fields across the highway, smelled the cane fires when the workers set them before harvesting. Kahuku was a plantation town, with rows of shacks and bungalows dominated, on the one hand, by the blackened exhaust spire of the Castle and Cook sugar mill but also, on the other, by the winglike roofline of the Nishi Hongwanji—the Buddhist church. It was a two-story building of bare, graying wood and grotesque carvings along its eaves and guarding the rails to the stairs. I didn't then know much about Buddhism, but its gargoyles impressed me with fear.

This was where I grew up, a place where my family, immigrants from southern Japan, had lived for three and a half generations. My ancestors came at the end of the nineteenth century, peasants displaced from their lands and exported as a diaspora of labor to help capitalize the industrialization of modern Japan. And, in a few weeks, we were to become immigrants again. Our future was to be on "the Mainland."

I'd heard the phrase many times, "the Mainland" being invoked like it was another paradise. Spoken at dinnertime, said out on the schoolyard, tossed in as a rhyme word in hopscotch and jump-rope games, it was nearly a religious mantra, something soteriological that signified potential and hope, saying that things would be better elsewhere—and soon. My playmates, cousins growing tired of hearing it from me so frequently, began to taunt, then spit it back as a curse. "You *go* Mainlan'," they'd say in the pidgin English that was our creole. As if it were a soul's leap into hell. But I was a believer, and I clung to its promise—a step across a transformational brink to redemption in some sociological afterlife. This was my future, a myth of deliverance.

That summer before we left, like every summer, there was a festival—the Bon Odori—a ritual that took place on the sandy parade ground, a kind of village square adjacent to the Hongwanji. There was also a mess hall for the plantation workers, a union hall, a Filipino barbershop, a Japanese barbershop, the tofu maker's shed, and the movie theater built for GIs during the war. A bit farther away, like petals off a sunflower, were the rows of worker houses.

A dance festival for the dead, the Bon Odori occurs during midsummer, near the time of the solstice, near the time, in rice-growing countries, of the harvest. The dances are based on motions derived from work—rice planting, coal mining, hoeing . . . And the songs that accompany them are also often about work. Bon Odori is celebrated in southern China, Japan, Hawai'i, and now along the West Coast, where Japanese immigrants have brought it to America. The idea is that the community dances all night long to earn good karma for the souls of the dead locked in a spiritual limbo that is a transitional paradise—it was Buddhism that invented the original twelve-step—so that souls will be freed and thus enabled to reach complete extinction, an escape from the cycle of birth and death, an escape from the carnal world altogether: nirvana. Symmetrically metaphysical in its logic, it is the most ingenious excuse for a block party I've ever heard of.

What I remember from that time is a set of images—people who were grimed, khaki-clad workers by day transformed by the festival into celebrants wearing white gowns and crisp, dark cotton jackets, everyone waving fans decorated with white cranes and the indecipherable emblems of calligraphy. There was a makeshift tower at the center of the square's sandy ground, and in the middle of it, on a linen-covered platform, gymnastic men took turns trouncing huge, barrel-like drums, while someone played a flute and someone else sang a rhythmic song about shoveling coal. All was lamplit. From time to time, the spinning dancers would shout refrains back to the singer. Women danced in concentric circles around the tower, slowly waving flagged sleeves as if they were huge fans attached to their arms. Within a circle of their own, the men bobbed and jerked like fish schooling in a contrapuntal dance. Pennants flapped and paper lanterns swung from wires strung overhead around the square. On a low platform near the temple, people brought their tributes— heaps of sacked rice, green and black pyramids of bottled liquor and soy sauce, and paper chains of individual and group pledges. I was given a papier-mâché bird that dandled from a stick and string. It twittered when you swung it. I was given a pink-and-yellow fan. It was the end of my childhood, and a peculiar joy filled the air like a wet wind bathing all of us in its erotic, tropical kiss.

That was my past—a memory of ecstatic commonality. An Edenic garden of cultural coherence.

It is important to say that, since then, I think my unconscious has worked to slowly merge what was the future and what had been the past in a way that says something about the tendency of subalterns to reimagine both along the lines that glorify and essentialize. This is the forgetting and revolutionary millenarianism, a kind of reification, that reproduces what has been made marginal, through complex interaction with cultures of dominance, as an archaic and mythic archive and, potentially, also as a totalizing system that, when engaged, particularly as lyric *teloi* in narrative schemes of transcendence, creates that illusory horizon of a future wherein ruptured colonial and regional identities are repaired and revitalized. For descendants of immigrant peoples, which most of us here are, if the future has been some fulfillment of potential, some graspable thing had after effort and in the condition of diaspora, if the future was "the Mainland" or "the West," then the past can have become some orgiastic cultural root in a prefragmentary, unisonant society, particularly in the cases where race, region, and ethnicity create elements of history and identity that resist assimilation or are excluded and silenced in the dominant culture. The past and the imagined future, then, can coalesce into writerly beliefs and narrative tendencies that function in a way similar to the functioning of a precritical, uninvestigated ethnic nationalism—a mythos for the saved and the excluded other.

This coalescence is troubling, yet, for those steeped in postcolonial studies, something quite recognizable. Homi Bhabha has described it as a practice that "inverts the axis of political discrimination by installing the excluded term at the center" (312). In ethnic literature, this is the claim of continuity and derivation from a precritical, mythic root—a metaphysical home that is the end point for any lyric of nostalgic, cultural praise. In writerly practices, it comes down to the fallacy of authenticity. It is possession of this essence that authenticates and makes recognizable a given work's tie to a people.

Postcolonial critics have identified this approach, this culturally *nationalistic* approach, as an aftereffect of the process in which a new political-cultural regime, after overturning the colonial power, reproduces the structure of colonial institutions and practices within colonized societies attempting decolonization under the sign of the revolutionary, the organic, and the *authentic*. What are deemed authentic in these configurations, therefore, are provisional political constructions of a society attempting to redefine itself with cultural referents recognizably antagonistic to the former powers or ruling set of values. This society creates a centrism, an essentialism along different alignments, reproducing its own version of the marginal and other in a process that, though purportedly revolutionary, is nevertheless hegemonic.

To cite from recent history, the Black Arts Movement of the sixties once elevated the firebrand Amiri Baraka and denounced the professorial Robert Hayden on these terms. The movement inspirited Gwendolyn Brooks to abandon formal approaches that smacked of canonicity and to adopt a more colloquial diction and folkloristic practices. Critically, it elevated Richard Wright while devaluing Ralph Ellison and cautioned James Baldwin to deemphasize and distance, in his public statements, the Jamesian influence on his fiction.

Since then, this kind of cultural nationalism has been effectively critiqued by a powerful cadre of black intellectuals who are well known. In African American intellectual circles, it is no longer easy to make claims about black authenticity regarding a literary work without appearing illiberal and underinformed.

Lamentably, "Asian American authenticity" has survived as a legitimate phrase and principle of investigation. It is frequently the very tool of the categorization, fostering a kind of historical vision that fills the past with stories of its victims, what Derek Walcott has called "a literature of recrimination and despair . . . [that] yellows into polemic or evaporates in pathos" (371). Used as a principle of canonical formation under the category of Asian American literature, it reproduces those centrist, essentializing tendencies of a cultural process that is one stage along a potential continuum of decolonization. Though useful for a brief cultural moment, it locks our literature into a reified past that stifles both learning and imagination. It is time to go further.

I have been back to Kahuku several times now. When I was ten, in order to firm up physically and maintain more island ways, I was sent from Los Angeles, where we'd moved, to live with an aunt in Honolulu. On a weekend trip to Kahuku, I visited to old village square where the Bon Odori festival had regularly taken place. It had long since ceased being held. When I went to the temple to inquire, I was told by a caretaker that the priest had retired and moved back to Japan, that the *sangha*, the parishioners, had all scattered and moved "to town" in Honolulu or else gone to the Mainland. My great-grandmother still lived nearby, but no one of the younger generations was left. The square and its surrounding buildings seemed a dry husk then, emptied of its grain.

And each time I've gone back, there has been less to see. Ten years ago, the last time I was there, the temple was boarded up, along with many of the shacks and bungalows. Some few of these were occupied by newcomers and even fewer by descendants of the original workers. I talked with a couple of them. They looked at my strange clothes and regarded my strange accent with suspicion. The strongest sense left of the old village and its people was in the yellowing temple moss over the sandy mounds of the graveyard on the promontory by the sea. And wind was scrubbing its wooden markers clean.

I think that the future, this soul's leap into a troubled metropolitanism, having arrived now, has shattered any misconceived harmonious totality that might have been the past. And the past will be fragments again, broken rice bowls left out on the saline ground of the cemetery by the sea. With Homi Bhabha, I envision this new future splitting the patriotic voice of unisonance, exiling the atavistic, ethnic past and its language of anterior belonging (see particularly Bhabha's comments [308–11] on Benedict Anderson's *Imagined Communities: Reflections on the Origin and Spread of Nationalism*). I see it opening to other histories and narrative subjects, becoming itself as American or European as it is regional and Asian, like the Argentinian literature Jorge Luis Borges saw as not only local but descended from "all of Western culture" (184). What remains to be accomplished, perhaps collectively, is a hybrid and transnational literature that will turn the past into questions for interrogating the future rather than maintain it as an Edenic garden of cultural coherence. We might then celebrate the bits and pieces left to us, not as fragments that we can piece together and reform into an archaic shape, Apollo or Ashikaga, but as elements for a new cultural mosaic, diaspora frescoes under a variegated spire somewhat freer from exploitative commerce and subaltern religious certainties, encrusted with porcelain shards polished by the sea.

Note: For words in the Hawaiian language, I am following the spelling given in Mary Kawena Pukui and Samuel H. Elbert's *Hawaiian Dictionary* (Honolulu: University of Hawai'i Press, 1986).

Works Cited

Bhabha, Homi K. "DissemiNation." In *Nation and Narration*, 293–312. London: Routledge, 1990.

Borges, Jorge Luis. "The Argentine Writer and Tradition." In *Labyrinths: Selected Stories and Other Writings*, 177–85. New York: New Directions, 1964.

Walcott, Derek. "The Muse of History." In *The Post-colonial Studies Reader*, edited by Bill Ashcroft, Gareth Griffiths, and Helen Tifflin, 370–74. London: Routledge, 1995.

HR 442

Redress

In April 1988, I was in the Senate gallery on hand for what I expected to be the final floor debate and passage of HR 442, legislation devised to compensate Japanese American survivors of the World War II relocation program. The idea was for the government to issue a formal apology and pay a financial settlement to anyone living who had suffered the forced evacuation and internment during World War II. Ceremoniously, the bill took its name after the all-Nisei Combat Team that had won numerous decorations for heroism on the battlefields of both Italy and France.

By now, everybody knows the story: How, in the aftermath of the Japanese bombing of Pearl Harbor in Hawai'i, President Franklin Roosevelt signed Executive Order 9066, sending 120,000 Japanese Americans into camps surrounded by barbed wire and run by the military, far removed from any populated areas; how the action was a result of racial prejudice and wartime hysteria; and how a good bunch of people were made to suffer greatly. Yet before the passage of HR 442, these facts were known mainly within the Japanese American community alone; the general public's attitude about them was either one of indifference, denial, or even mild hostility. Moreover, Japanese Americans themselves had to overcome their own powerful feelings of shame and fear that had remained from those times.

On the afternoon just before the bill's final passage, I was upstairs in the balcony overlooking the Senate floor, listening to a mannerly but nettlesome debate between Spark Matsunaga from Hawai'i and Jesse Helms of North Carolina. Matsunaga, as its author, had been taking the measure through debate, all largely tributary. But, at the last minute, Jesse Helms had proposed an unfriendly "Pearl Harbor Amendment."

Though Helms agreed that history, in its twenty-twenty hindsight, has shown that the evacuation and relocation was a mistake, he still wanted an amendment to stipulate that no funds be appropriated until the Japanese government compensated the families of the men and women who were killed at Pearl Harbor on December 7, 1941.

"I owe this to the families of our military personnel at Pearl Harbor who were either killed or injured," Helms was saying, pitting redress against memories of America's war dead.

We were still being associated with Japanese war atrocities. My own grandfather, American-born, had been imprisoned for a time because of this kind of prejudice and my father, all of seventeen then, had shipped out in 1944 as part of a contingent to replace Nisei troops lost in European combat. Despite all this, Helms could still put us back into the frame of that old story. It was the Japanese American version of the Scottsboro Boys.

I thought about this for a while, glancing at the others sitting with me in the gallery that afternoon. There were a couple of dozen other Japanese Americans from different parts of the country. They represented three generations: Nisei, second generation; Sansei, third generation; and Yonsei, fourth generation. And they all had something to do with redress. We were quiet, waiting to hear how Senator Matsunaga would reply.

Matsunaga, now deceased, was over seventy then, and the issue on which this bill was based had been an important one to him for a long time. He had been a lieutenant in the army during World War II and saw combat in Italy, fighting alongside other Japanese American soldiers whose families were imprisoned in the United States. His colleague and cosponsor of the bill, Hawai'i Senator Daniel Inouye, had been through a similar experience, losing an arm in combat. They were American war heroes. Even Senator Helms, speaking in opposition to the bill, had to acknowledge this. He referred to their military service, their "valor," and made protestations about how much he respected them.

Up in the gallery, I had been hoping for the scene below to add up to a closing moment. For over ten years a "redress

173

movement" had been building along several fronts. It pushed to educate the American public about the internment of Japanese Americans, pushed for federal legislation to grant monetary compensation, and petitioned the courts to overturn old Supreme Court cases that upheld the legality of the evacuation of 1942.

In April 1984, a federal district court in San Francisco had granted a special *coram nobis* petition brought by a team of young Japanese American attorneys. They had asked that the case known as *United States v. Korematsu* be set aside, that Fred Korematsu, a Nisei who had been convicted for refusing to comply with the evacuation order in 1942, be declared innocent and his record expunged. The new federal decision did that. Subsequently, in 1986, a district judge in Seattle ruled favorably in the matter of another *coram nobis* petition regarding *United States v. Hirabayashi,* a similar 1942 Supreme Court case. These were historic victories for the Japanese American community and personal ones for the two Nisei men then convicted for refusing to obey the evacuation orders. The cases galvanized community and media attention, educated the public, and gave Japanese Americans at large a feeling of vindication.

In October 1987, the National History Museum of the Smithsonian Institute had opened a major exhibit, scheduled for perpetual display, entitled "A More Perfect Union: Japanese Americans and the U.S. Constitution." It dramatized both the evacuation itself and the heroic war contributions of Japanese American soldiers, spotlighting national media attention on what had been an almost forgotten episode and made a case against the government for the World War II civil rights violations of its Japanese American citizens. Thousands of Japanese Americans from all over the country had converged on Washington for a series of public ceremonies, reunions, and private receptions commemorating the event.

Finally, and perhaps most significantly, a push for federal legislation grew out of a long-term exercise in American democracy—something the Japanese American community had, ever since the war years, a collectively troubled belief in. For over a decade, there had been a tempestuous political campaign run from within the membership of the Japanese American Citizens' League (JACL), a national political organization, by former evacuees like Edison Uno, Min Yasui, and John Tateishi who wanted to push Congress to make official amends for the internment years. Uno, a Nisei on the education faculty at San Francisco State University, had long been an activist in the cause to accomplish some restitution to Japanese Americans for what they had suffered. During the late 1960s and throughout the 1970s, Uno had come repeatedly to lobby the JACL National Convention to introduce a resolution asking that the U.S. government provide reparations to Japanese Americans.

In 1970 Uno drafted a resolution calling for the government to make an official apology and to pay monetary compensation, and thereby authored what had become the two fundamental tenets of Japanese American redress. Given the Elizabethan-sounding title of "A Requital Supplication," Uno's resolution became the focus for a national campaign within the JACL. But the membership remained bitterly divided about the issue for eight more years. There were many who still suffered from a great psychological turmoil and social fears from their years in the internment camps. They found it hard to even mention those times, much less push Congress for any significant legislation.

"They really had been thinking of themselves as second-class citizens," said John Tateishi, who became the inheritor of the movement Uno had started. A well-spoken and smartly dressed man, Tateishi is the Sansei, a third-generation Japanese American, who became national chairman of the JACL Redress Committee in 1976. I spoke to him at a reception sponsored by the National History Museum.

"The Nisei were reluctant. It took a lot of discussion amongst ourselves. A *process* had to take place. People needed to voice reservations. They had to focus on the issue of our acceptance as citizens in this country. They had to face the fact that they really had been thinking of themselves as *second-class* and conquer that sense, quite deep-rooted, within themselves. They had to come out of a profound dread of bringing back the psychological pain. These were people who couldn't even talk to their wives or husbands about the internment, not to mention their kids."

Grace Uyehara, a Nisei social worker from Philadelphia, served with Tateishi on the Redress Committee and eventually succeeded him as national coordinator. A smallish woman in her seventies, she echoed some of his observations when I spoke to her.

"We were raised not to expose feelings," she said to me over coffee in a Washington restaurant. "Do you know *haji*?" She used the Japanese word for "shame."

"We felt something must've been wrong with *us*, that we were the unwanted people. It was hard for us to admit we were a despised people, a rejected people," she told me. "That was the toughest. After that, we had to create the network and realize we had a responsibility to change the direction of our society— not only American society, but the direction *within* the Japanese American community. We had some unfinished business to attend to. The resolution forced us to deal with the feeling that it wasn't *us*, but that it was American society that was wrong."

The Salt Lake City JACL Convention in 1978 passed a two-part resolution calling for a governmental apology and a financial payment to survivors. It asked that $25,000 be paid to each individual who went through the internment. The demand for the $25,000 drew immediate media interest. The JACL began attracting wider public attention to the issue. Overall, even though the membership remained regionally and politically fractured, the resolution itself created a public sense that there was now a unified voice coming out of Japanese America.

In January 1979, armed with their resolution, officials from the JACL finally approached the Nikkei Caucus for help in devising a scheme for accomplishing legislation. The Nikkei Caucus referred to the small group of four Japanese American legislators then in Washington. It was made up of Senators Matsunaga and Inouye of Hawai'i and Representatives Norman Mineta and Robert Matsui of California. The legislation was personally important to each of them. Matsunaga said, "I had relatives who were confined in those camps." Mineta and Matsui had, as children, both been victims of the wartime internment. "I owe it to my buddies," Inouye had said when I'd visited him, gesturing to the battalion flag of the all-Nisei 442nd Regimental Combat Team in the corner of his Senate office.

The group met many times over a four-month period and assessed the difficulty of introducing such legislation without any other preparation than the JACL resolution. Senator Daniel Inouye proposed an idea to create a commission that would study the matter and hold public hearings throughout the country. By thus exposing the issue to national and local media, they hoped to gather support for the Japanese American point of view. The committee would then give a final report to the House Judiciary Committee and make official recommendations. Perhaps one of those recommendations would be for legislation.

When I visited Senator Inouye in his Senate office back in 1987, he emphasized planning and consensus-building.

"A massive education job was necessary," Inouye said. "The majority of Americans are only vaguely aware of what happened to Japanese Americans during World War II."

Many colleagues in the Senate were also ignorant. "I tried to convince them by speaking to each one personally," Matsunaga told me. "They didn't know! Not being of Japanese ancestry or close to anyone who was, it took some time to explain it to them."

"I was convinced," Inouye said, "that if we came up with a measure *flat out*, it would not be accepted. In order to make it succeed, it had to be a national effort, not just an effort pursued by Americans of Japanese ancestry. So I suggested that the commission be made up not of Japanese Americans but of a cross-section of distinguished Americans. It would be a weak case if it was just a movement supported by one narrow segment of our community. This had to be a national effort. It had to be a recommendation coming from the people of the United States saying clearly that a wrong had been committed against a small segment of Americans and that something should be done about it. I thought that approach would be better than a Japanese American group saying '*They* have done *us* wrong, therefore you owe *us* something, and therefore you should *do* something for us.' And so you pit a small group against a nation. Now, this other way, the nation is coming out and saying, 'You picked on that small group. You shouldn't have done that.'"

The Inouye strategy was implemented. According to Mineta, it took two Congresses, but the Presidential Commission on Wartime Relocation and Internment of Civilians completed its work in June 1983, having conducted numerous public hearings throughout the West Coast and in Washington, DC. It heard testimony from hundreds of citizens who had been interned during the war. These people spoke repeatedly and with great emotion about their experiences, many of them for the first time in their lives. The hearings were a momentous and catalytic event for the Japanese American community, and, for the first time since the evacuation of 1942, a story about them was making national and local news.

The Commission's report to the House Judiciary Committee in December 1982 was a spectacular victory for the redress movement. Given the suggestive title "Personal Justice Denied," the report stated that the wartime internment not only was unwarranted but was a result of "race prejudice, war hysteria and a failure of political leadership." It described suffering and deprivation in tar-paper barracks, mass living in conditions that humiliated and prevented normal family intimacy. The Commission's recommendations urged that redress be legislated and that a sum of $20,000 be paid to each survivor.

The Nikkei Caucus then busied itself lining up support within both houses of Congress. Over the next five years, a team of lobbyists from the JACL joined with them, recruiting into the cause members like Dick Cheney and Jim Wright, senators like Bill Bradley. "We made it an issue of national honor," Matsunaga said.

Under the leadership of Speaker Jim Wright, the 100th Congress ceremoniously passed redress legislation on the day of the Constitutional Bicentennial, September 17, 1987. Democratic leaders like Tom Foley, Tony Coelho, and Barney Frank had fought for it, and, when it came to the House floor for discussion, some of the speeches given in support were poetic tributes and lyric testimonies.

"I would like . . . to indicate to all of you perhaps what it was like to be an American citizen in 1942 if you happened to be of Japanese ancestry," Congressman Matsui had said, speaking from the floor of the House. "My mother and father, who were in their twenties, were both born and raised in Sacramento, California, so they were American citizens by birth. They were trying to start their careers. They had a child who was six months old. They had a home like any other American. They had a car. My father had a little produce business with his brother. For some reason because of Pearl Harbor in 1942, their lives and their futures were shattered. They were given 72 hours' notice that they had to leave their home, their neighborhood, abandon their business, and show up at the Memorial Auditorium which is in the heart of Sacramento and then be taken, like cattle in trains, to the Tule Lake Internment Camp. My father was not able to talk about this subject for over forty years. . . . I was a six-month-old child born in this country."

Norman Mineta chose to read a letter his father had written from an internment camp to friends, describing what he felt as he left his home.

"I looked at Santa Clara's streets from the train over the subway," Mineta said, quoting his father. "I thought this might be the last look at my loved home city. My heart almost broke, and suddenly hot tears came pouring out, and the whole family cried out, could not stop, until we were out of our loved country." Mineta had wept and his voice choked as he read. "We lost our homes, we lost our businesses, we lost our farms," the Congressman said in summation, "but worst of all we lost our basic human rights."

When the roll call vote was taken, redress had passed the House 243–141.

Within the Senate, Matsunaga had introduced a similar bill and signed on seventy-six cosponsors, including Republican conservatives Orrin Hatch, Alan Simpson, and Ted Stevens. "He made this almost a personal crusade," his colleague Inouye told me. Fellow Democrats like John Glenn, Paul Simon, and Alan Cranston also helped give the bill its avid bipartisan support. Though it was originally scheduled immediately after passage of the House bill, the Senate's version of redress came up for discussion in April of the following year. At the time, Matsunaga worried briefly about a threat of filibustering from Jesse Helms. A vote for cloture, a procedure to limit discussion to forty-eight hours, prevented this, however, and insured that opposition would not be effective.

But in the Senate gallery that afternoon, I could still feel an atmosphere of worry. Helms's opposition still struck a nerve. I felt the specter of an old fear.

In the first row was Mike Masaoka, a deeply tanned and gray-haired Nisei man in his seventies. At the time of the war, Masaoka was national secretary of the Japanese American Citizens' League, a kind of national Kiwanis Club for Japanese Americans or, to be more complimentary, an NAACP for Americans of Japanese descent. After Pearl Harbor, he was one of a few Japanese American leaders called in to meet with officials from the Roosevelt administration. Masaoka, then in his late twenties, had publicly urged compliance with the relocation order.

"We were misled by the government," he had told me when I spoke to him. "We were desperate, you see. If the army was going to move us out, if they had to come in with bayonets, what would be the reaction of the American people? We decided to cooperate rather than have the army come after us. We sat down, we tried to work it out thinking that the more we cooperated with them, the more livable they'd make things in camp. It was a question of survival then."

Listening to Masaoka speak, I found myself feeling empathetic with his anxieties. It is deeply ingrained among many minorities that we will not be understood, that our truths will never be part of the national truth, that we are still second-class. It has ensured our silence about injustice many times. It was clear to me that Masaoka had felt powerless in 1942, called before Congress and to private meetings with the military as a leader of the Japanese American community that, as a whole, was under powerful suspicion.

"I keep looking over the facts, over and over again. I talked to the generals, the FBI agents, and other people whom we cooperated with, and I'm convinced that the alternative would have been disastrous. We would have had absolutely no future in this country."

Redress, for Masaoka and others, was a way to get the story told right, the political means to accomplish a wish, said over and again, that the evacuation and relocation episode *be known,* that the story no longer be confined within our own community.

"I want the American people to understand what happened to us," Masaoka said. "I want our history written down."

Helms's misplaced jingoism stood in the way. He rose from his desk on the Senate floor, finishing his statements.

"I have heard from a lot of survivors of American fighting

men who were killed in Pearl Harbor on December 7, 1941, and they say, 'How about us?'" Helms said.

But there was a new story out there about Japanese Americans now, and the senator from North Carolina seemed to be the only one still trying to tell the old one.

"This amendment is totally unacceptable," Senator Matsunaga replied. "It presumes that we Americans of Japanese ancestry had something to do with the bombing of Pearl Harbor. That is absolutely false. In this bill we are trying to distinguish between Japanese Americans and Japanese. The amendment would obscure this distinction."

Matsunaga had said it forcefully, succinctly. Behind his statements were all his accomplishments, the Nikkei Caucus, the emotional speeches of scores of his colleagues already made on the House and Senate floors endorsing the bill, and, finally, about ten years of a national political movement.

It was over. Matsunaga and Helms, both standing, locked eyes, and then Helms dropped back into his seat, mopping his brow with a handkerchief. Matsunaga remained standing. A motion to table Helms's "Pearl Harbor Amendment" passed 91–4.

The roll call vote followed. A buzzer went off, and the entire Senate assembled. One by one, from Bill Bradley, the most athletic, to Howard Metzenbaum, the most stooped, senators glided and shuffled to the voting table at the front of the hall. Inouye and Matsunaga stood alongside one another and shook hands with everyone. After the announcement of the final vote (69–27), Matsunaga grabbed Inouye's hand and raised it with his. Old-timers, they blew sentimental aloha kisses to the Nisei gallery.

I was full of my own dreamy sentimentalisms then, trying to rhapsodize myself into the emotional center of this story. When I spoke with the pool of newspaper reporters later, I was critical of their descriptions of Senator Matsunaga as a kind of American Don Quixote finalizing a crusade, achieving his dream. I said that the characterization was too romantic: "It implies impossibility." Borrowing a phrase from a poem of Coleridge's, I said what Matsunaga had done was more like maintaining "a quiet ministry of faith."

The next day, I read my remarks as leads from syndicated

news stories in Knight-Ridder, Gannett, and Copley News Service papers all over America.

"Passage of this bill has freed me from a burden I've carried for over forty years," Congressman Matsui told me not long afterwards. "It just *had* to be done."

When I left the Senate late in the afternoon, a wonderful light drizzled down through all the trees on the street outside. Redress had brought about a transformation of awareness in the national consciousness about Japanese Americans. The movement had successfully established their innocence and loyalty during World War II and refocused public opinion. Finally, the unique legislation accomplished by Matsunaga and the Nikkei Caucus was evidence that, after almost half a century, the official story about the evacuation and internment, one that had been clouded in fear, shame, and suspicion, had finally been corrected.

"It's all over," said Matsui. "We can talk about it. It's no longer something we should be ashamed of."

Hope Alive

Writers at the Unconvention

"Go on, Jesse!" Harvard philosopher Cornel West shouted from his bar seat, gesticulating at the television screen that showed Jesse Jackson speaking live before the Democratic Convention across town. West, the novelist Toni Morrison, and I were relaxing over drinks after our own event as part of the "Unconvention," a slate of more intimate venues arranged to complement the "big tent" show at Chicago's United Center. Along with novelists Bharati Mukherjee and Richard Ford, playwright David Henry Hwang, and poet Sandra Cisneros, we'd been brought together by Senator Bill Bradley and the City of Chicago Human Relations Commission for "A Conversation: Race and the Creative Imagination."

Skinny as Oz's scarecrow, his black hair brushed up in a moderate Afro, and wearing a natty, three-piece blue pinstripe suit, West was concentrating all the attention in the hotel bar, punctuating Jackson's dramatic speech with musical, vocalized enthusiasm that worked like cymbal crashes and thumps from a bass drum: "That's right, brother!" and "Uh-huh! You onnit" and "You know it's right!"

Jackson, of course, had been expected to endorse the current, quite centrist Democratic Party agenda, but, in a moment of high oratory, the old Rainbow Coalitionist could not resist invoking the party's legacy of struggle and protest. "We serve a mighty God!" Jackson called, bringing his speech to its final crescendos of hyperbole and drama.

"Jesse's on to it now!" West proclaimed. He spun in his seat, nodded his head and smiled broadly at Morrison, the distinguished and divalike Nobel laureate in literature, seated in a tulip chair next to him. She sipped her drink and laughed, saying, "Oh yeah, that Jesse!"

That afternoon, the 1,200-seat theater at the Field Museum on the shore of Lake Michigan filled up completely with a predominately black audience that also included Asians, a few Latinos, and many white, most of them wearing delegate badges. I noticed opera soprano Jessye Norman sitting in the fifth row. Someone whispered that Illinois senator Carol Mosely Brown had arrived. Chinese American poet Li-Young Lee, black-nationalist poet Haki Madhubuti, and Chicano poet Luis Rodriguez took seats near the front. The seven of us—Sandra Cisneros had to drop out at the last minute—took the stage. Then Bradley addressed the audience.

This was the man who had, in another life, shot down the Lakers' hopes and boosted the Willis Reed-led Knicks to victory in the 1972 NBA Finals with two last-minute jumpers and a series of clutch free throws. I had watched these feats in complete misery in my dorm lounge at Pomona College. More recently, I had seen him on the day the Senate passed HR 442—the redress bill of 1988 that made an official apology and paid financial compensation to Japanese Americans evacuated and placed in concentration camps during World War II. I was in the Senate balcony that day and remember that he was one of the first in the chamber to congratulate Senators Spark Matsunaga and Daniel Inouye of Hawai'i, the bill's initial sponsors. I also remember that Bradley was the first important congressional figure to speak out against Jesse Helms's attacks on the NEA.

Now, the senator spoke amiably about his growing up in a small town in Missouri, isolated from racial issues but not without compassion for his father, a disabled man who became the town's banker. Bradley called for racial healing and an open dialogue on race, and then began with a question for Morrison and Hwang.

"How did race figure as a motivation for you to begin to write?" Bradley asked.

Morrison was silent for a moment, then answered by talking about her first novel, *The Bluest Eye*. She announced that part of her motivation behind writing it was to write for an audience of young black women like herself. Nobody up until that time was addressing books to black women, she felt, and she wanted to do that specifically. Part of doing that involved creating a character Morrison hated completely, the blue-eyed antiheroine of the novel whom she made the embodiment of evil and the recipient of her social revenge. But she soon realized that she couldn't do that, that art wasn't the place to get her revenge. So Morrison began to create more multidimensional characters and moral complexities reflective of society's ambiguities.

Hwang, winner of a Tony for *M. Butterfly*, and author of several commercial screenplays, said that when he was a child, every time an Asian face came on the television screen he would switch the channel because he knew it would make him feel bad. The Asian characters were always ludicrous and had nothing to do with him or his father or any of the Asian Americans he knew and grew up with. So, when he began writing he worked hard to create other kinds of Asian characters, characters he himself might feel better about, whether they were exemplary or not, whether they were good guys or bad guys or pretty girls or warrior women. He wanted to give them all more dimension.

Bradley asked the rest of us to describe the first time we noticed someone, perhaps ourselves, being treated differently because of race.

"It was probably something that I did," Richard Ford said, striking a note of high candor. Winner of this year's Pulitzer for his novel *Independence Day* (no relation to the movie), Ford is a man whose thin, reedlike appearance reminded me of the expert gambler's in a TV Western, or the taciturn master swordsman's in Kurosawa's classic film *The Seven Samurai*. He explained how he grew up in Jackson, Mississippi, where he never got to know any black children until he was an adolescent and noticed that their schools were different from his. He admitted he'd been ignorant until the civil rights movement sensitized him to the problems of a segregated society. I admired his not trying to pave over the past, even his own personal one.

West described a time in Sacramento when he was 14. He was brought by a Caucasian classmate to the white side of town to a public pool in order to learn to swim. The moment West dived into the pool, everyone else, scores of people, just jumped out of it, he said, as if he had polluted the water with his color. Later, the workers at the pool drained it.

"This only heightened the absurdity," West said, reaching his hands out to the audience, taking a long, eloquent, and entertaining excursus into the black capacity for handling "adversity and absurdity." The audience applauded and laughed, charmed by West's verbal riffings, his rim shots of quotation and aphorism, his dancelike performance of the English language.

Fiction writer and Berkeley professor Bharati Mukherjee, her melodic, alto voice rising, explained how she was raised in privilege and isolation in Calcutta and never knew she was "a color" until she came to the University of Iowa. There, she said, she encountered "football culture" and folks walking up to her in the supermarkets to touch her sari and proclaim "how beautiful" she was in her native costume. Again, the audience laughed.

I cited an anecdote from my college years, when a literature professor, the Los Angeles poet Bert Meyers, pulled me aside after my first class with him. I'd been a sullen presence during the evening's discussion, a poetry workshop dominated by a long-haired, bearded man smelling of patchouli oil. Meyers asked me to walk partway across campus with him. He stopped under a street lamp to light his pipe. "I know why you're so angry," Meyers said, jabbing the stem of his pipe into my chest. "Your parents were in those camps."

He meant the relocation camps of World War II where 120,000 Japanese-Americans were evacuated from the West Coast in 1942. He'd been a high school student at Marshall in Los Angeles, and, he told me, one day in May during his junior year, all the Japanese American students were suddenly gone. Five guys from his gymnastics team. A guy who was his best friend. Meyers was saying that he knew a story that burned within me and which the culture had forced us to be silent about for a generation and a half. He said he would help me with it. I followed him. He freed a story within me that had been silence. That's how I began to want to be a poet.

As the discussion turned to the issue of empathy and the ability to imagine others of another race, Hwang argued for the patient method of trying to listen to others' concerns, opinion, and fears—not necessarily agreeing with them or sharing them—but trying to "get it." Morrison proclaimed the need for serious fiction to create characters that were not "one-dimensional like life and politics." (That got a big laugh, too.) She wanted "the three-dimensionality of literature," characters of all colors and ethnicities who possessed good and evil both, so that we could "broaden the conversation" regarding race and "say what's kept out of it over there" at the United Center.

My own comments dwelt on a notation of asserting "full citizenship," urging everyone to keep in mind that cultural work still needed to be done, that there was a need to build identity from within, based on the individual specificities of a life rather than some massive, mainstream notion of a "norm," and to assert that identity in cultural expression—that a Chicano poet and a Native American poet proclaim our national identity as much as or more than any canonical "tradition" approved by the academic mandarins. As a nation, we need to construct models of plurality and multiplicity rather than monoliths of commonality that occlude difference and silence unique histories.

Ford spoke of the importance of "respecting your characters" of whatever race. Hwang added that, as a playwright, he knew that he'd have to listen to his characters 50 percent of the time so that they would listen to him 50 percent of the time. West, who might begin a sentence quoting Herman Melville and Franz Kafka but end it citing something from the secular scripture of jazz (and whose invocation of John Coltrane's Sufi spiritual "A Love Supreme" brought down the house), asked the audience to change themselves from within first, before they asked others to change.

Then West turned the discussion toward the problems of political power and the distribution of wealth, empowerment, and education. He suggested that the reason the convention discussion about race was so bland was because there was no popular movement from the outside putting pressure on the delegates.

"Do you realize," he said, his tone picking up volume and urgency, his body jerking and swaying like a Baptist preacher, "that, today, there are more poor, more unemployed, than in 1968, and that we have literally gone backwards in terms of economic development among the working class? But the reason we talked about those things in '68 and not now is because in '68 the people were in the streets and demonstrating!"

In closing, Bradley talked about the value of "giving up privilege" as he did when he was an NBA player. He knew that, though he wasn't nearly the best player on the team, not even the second- or third-best, he was getting endorsement opportunities from the corporations simply because he was white, and he didn't feel good about that. So he declined, consistently, throughout his career to make these endorsements. Praising the senator, Morrison suggested that his gesture needed to he universalized throughout society, so that no one would accrue privilege by race.

We left, stating the hope that more discussions might emerge in the future, not exclusively among writers again, but that the delegates and politicians might take heart from our effort and regain the confidence to seriously broaden their conversations to include race relations in a manner that would be empowering rather than divisive. A step might be to listen to the people whose lives are affected by problems of race and stereotypes; who are struggling to create identities free of denigrating labels; who, as much as anyone, seek to create lives of dignity and passion.

I think it was important for the audience, particularly the delegates in attendance, to see that thoughtful people could lend their goodwill and contribute a measure of cultural prestige to the serious discussion of painful racial issues. Though there were political as well as racial differences among us, our discussion remained reasonable and open throughout, even affable and entertaining at times. There seemed the glimmer of the Old World intelligentsia about the panel, or the precolonial council of village elders. With only one of us there, it would have devolved into the unctuous "celebrity interview" and focused too much on the trivial. I realized, therefore, that this panel was something quite special, since the convening of cultural intellectuals is rare as an American public event. My own hope is that this was the start of something that could become a familiar style of forum making. This time, it was just as much fun for me to listen as it was to have my say.

On the warm, humid evening before, Sandra Cisneros, the current MacArthur fellow and author of *The House on Mango Street*, a collection of moving vignettes about life in Chicago's Latino neighborhoods, wanted to walk back down Michigan Avenue to our hotel, so I accompanied her. Cisneros told me stories of her growing up in Chicago, of moving seven times around town during her childhood before they found a place where they could stay awhile. She saw the city dressed up in new flowers in the parkways and medians, and she wondered where all the money was coming from, how long the pretty flowers would last before they were stolen. She was going through a deep, personal grief, and it was a little hard for her to be back in the city where she grew up. She told me how she worked for two years answering phones for the gas company—"in that building over there," she said, pointing to a granite façade across the boulevard that was streaming with cars and buses.

"Hey, look," she said. "Look at those beautiful chandeliers up there!" She pointed to some winking yellow lights like amber flames about three stories up. I felt drops of water sprinkling me.

"Is it raining or are they only washing windows?" Cisneros said, looking up at the lower building above us.

"Oh," she said. "It's window washers. See the cables?" She pointed again.

"I can't walk through this city without thinking of all the workers like I was," she said. "Answering phones, washing windows, delivering the food, making the food . . ."

Then I thought of the world of chandeliers. I suggested we go there, see if we could get in the building and look up at them.

"Oh, *yesss*," she said, smiling, grabbing my arm, picking up walking speed as we went with the light, feeling the puffs of late summer wind billow and slap through our thin clothing, petals of window washing raining down, the chandelier lights above us little blossoms of promise over the streets we struggled, just slightly, to cross.

Lost in Place

Longing for the Brave New World of L.A.

One Labor Day some years ago, I was sitting at the dining table at my place in Eugene, Oregon, gazing out of the picture window over the front lawn at my two boys, Hudson and Alex, as they took turns splashing around in a wading pool with a small group of their friends. It was Alex's seventh birthday party, and his mother had arranged for about a dozen other boys to come over and celebrate with him. It was hot in Oregon, and the children would queue up in the most well-behaved manner and then yell like rioters as they took long jumps, triple jumps, and belly flops into the tiny pool I'd filled with a garden hose earlier that morning. Alex was loudest of all, improvising a variety of whoops, giggles, and *Ohh, mannnnn!*'s as he took his sailing dives into the grass-specked water.

"Watch, Dad! Watch!" he'd hell, and then take a sprint toward the inflated skirts of the pool, leaping and splashing down, showering that summery water on his brother and their playmates.

This might have been happiness itself, but, from the inside house, gazing up from the book of poems I was trying to read, I had the acute feeling that much of this was wrong. Except for my two sons, the hair on all the other boys was blond, or towheaded straw blond—but blond. No one else seemed bothered by this or even to notice—not my wife, who is brunette, not my in-laws, who are also brown-haired. But it drove me into an instant panic. And I began to feel angry.

I grew up among a mix of peoples both in Hawai'i and in Los Angeles. Born in Hawai'i, I spent my childhood among Hawaiians and Filipinos and Samoans on the North Shore of O'ahu before my family settled in Los Angeles in the late fifties. I went to primary school in midtown L.A., to fifth and sixth grades in Woodland Hills, and to junior high school and high school in Gardena.

We moved first to a neighborhood of apartment houses and old bungalows that housed a mix of peoples who arrived there from Jalisco or Hattiesburg, Honolulu or Hong Kong. I heard jump-rope rhymes in Japanese and the English of Southern blacks, I heard hopscotch songs from Sonora and Seoul, and I played cat's cradle with my cousins, who gave me elaborate instructions in Hawaiian pidgin English. In Woodland Hills, my family had moved on up, and that meant most of the other families in our neighborhood were white, and I felt racially isolated and socially quite lonely for a couple of years. We moved to Gardena, therefore, where there are a ton of Japanese Americans and their grocery stores, nurseries, auto-body and transmission-repair shops, and teriyaki taco stands. I was home, Jim, and, in junior high, I had a ball learning the boogaloo and the Philly dog from the black kids bused in from Compton.

By high school, I dressed and talked "blackJap" while beginning to read deeply in the literature books our white teachers assigned to us. But only the Jewish kids would talk about books, so on Friday nights, rather than rumble with recidivist car-club boys or take a date to a Chicano dance hall, I drove over to the Fairfax district with my new friends, who introduced me to their cousins who went to Hollywood High and University High. Rather than chase the waves for good surf in Hermosa Beach, I started feeling comfortable hanging out at kosher delis, the Samuel French Bookstore, all-night diners and art-movie theaters, talking J. D. Salinger and LeRoi Jones and Luis Buñuel with kids who reminisced about Hebrew school and their bar and bat mitzvahs.

When I got bored, I went to hear jazz at Spanky's on Washington with my black friends. Or I went to the Lighthouse down in Hermosa with a white saxophone player I knew. At home, my family still did things Hawaiian- and Japanese-style—no shoes in the house, gas-station calendars from Kahuku Plantation, rice with every meal, chopsticks instead of forks, and vacations in Vegas that I avoided. And, within myself, none of this seemed especially strange. Yet I was aware I was crossing borders, that

I couldn't carry with me too many signs as I traveled from one neighborhood or group of folks to another. A cultural slip could cancel my ticket-of-transit. I had become a magpie, an ethnic chameleon, a junior-league multiculti before the fact.

My own children, though, were growing up in a very different kind of world. It was all white, and, I began to think, I'd made a big mistake. How would they know about others? And how would they relate to me?

Last month, my son Alex asked for some photographs of himself as a baby. He needed them for a bulletin-board project his fifth-grade class was doing. The idea was to scramble up a bunch of baby pictures with current ones and make everyone try to match the baby with the fifth-grader.

I rummaged around in the family albums and came up with a set of snapshots of Alex in Hawai'i, Houston, and Missouri. He swam with other kids in small *keiki* ("sprout") ponds by the ocean in Hawai'i, sat alone in a fire engine and wore a fireman's hat in Houston, and waved a tiny American flag at his younger brother by the forsythia bush in Missouri.

"Oh no," Alex groaned. "This isn't going to work."

"Why not?" I asked.

"Because no one else in my class is Asian American," Alex said. "All people have to do is choose the baby with the black hair, and they know it's me. There's no mystery and there's no fun."

"Well," I said, improvising, "you're just unique, man. That's all."

"I'm tired of being unique, Dad," Alex answered. "I'm tired of being easy to pick out." I had to admit I could understand his feelings. Being different wears you down.

Eugene had been a choice of ours, my wife's and mine. She is from here and grew up feeling supported and secure. We came because we knew the schools would be good, because it was a way to give our children grandparents and an extended family, provide the base of familial and geographic stability she'd enjoyed as a child, as opposed to all the shifting around that I had done. It was safe, cheap, and manageable for the middle-class people we were becoming.

We'd met in college, at Pomona near Los Angeles, and fell in love sharing our family histories. On her father's side, my wife is descended from Mennonite farmers who moved to Oregon from Manitoba, where they had lived on a commune like the ones they'd been forced from in Ukraine and in Holland before that. The Mennonites are both a religious sect and an ethnic group. On her mother's side, my wife is descended from North Dakota Quakers who moved to Oregon after the Depression. My people are southern Japanese peasants and samurai who, dispossessed of their farms and swords, immigrated to Hawai'i at the end of the nineteenth century to work as laborers, union organizers, and storekeepers in the sugarcane fields and pine-apple plantations. We recognized each other as children of a world diaspora.

She played the violin and studied music, while I set about trying to build a career as a poet, writing largely about the Japanese American past. I found work in universities far-flung from L.A.—in Texas, Missouri, and Orange County—with colleagues schooled in literature but ignorant and, I thought, scornful of the kinds of histories my wife and I had sprung from. We lived in Hawai'i for a while, then I was offered a job at the University of Oregon. It seemed an end to our wanderings.

But eventually I realized that, as an academic inducted into what Caribbean poet Derek Walcott once called "white fellow-ships," I had become too far removed from the world of urban ethnic and cultural diversity from which I had sprung. Living in Eugene had been happy enough from my family, and, mostly, for me in it, but some years ago I began to have problems with the town.

I grew bored with the two or three "good" restaurants, the commercial cineplexes in the shopping malls, and the company of blandness that characterizes the generally suburban life I'd fallen into. I lamented that there were hardly any black people, Latinos, or Asian Americans—no brothers and sisters at all.

At faculty mixers hosted by the dean, I zoned out. I faked my way through neighborhood get-togethers and receptions at my kids' elementary school. I was getting angry and depressed. Everyone around me talked mainly about fly-fishing, pasta salads, and summer classical-music festivals. Even the style and rhythm of their speech wore me down. It was all so complacent, untroubled, so blandly innocent of woe, that I resorted to moviegoing for my dose of the real. I shouted in celebration at Sam Jackson's soliloquy in *Pulp Fiction.*

"We need that man in Eugene!" I yelled. The good people in the dark theater, stunned and embarrassed for me, stayed politely silent.

Failing to stand guard over myself at backyard lawn and sundeck parties, I'd kid the sweet neighbors, the colleagues and their wives dressed in cottons from L. L. Bean, try switching subjects, and even risk putting them down. When things like the L.A. riots, Spike Lee's *Malcolm X*, or the Million Man March made the news, acquaintances in India Import skirts would start saying something mildly disparaging and then stop, realizing my sympathies were different.

Recently, a woman I recognized from the PTA stopped me in the popcorn line at the movies.

"Oh, Mr. Hongo," she said, "I'm so glad I ran into you. I've been meaning to ask if you'd come and speak about your native culture to my son's third-grade class?"

"Oh," I said disingenuously. "You mean gangs?"

I was becoming cruel. People now saw me as dangerous. I got quieter, meditating, reading. I distanced myself at the university, isolated myself within the town. I realized that, along with my own misanthropy, it was the ignorance and social homogeneity up here that was the cause of all this. I felt like I'd had a revelation. I told my acquaintances in Eugene that I could no longer tolerate being the only person of color they knew. We dropped each other and I started feeling better.

Now, I nod to folks, but barely anyone engages my conversation. People in the supermarkets assume I'm a foreign student on academic sojourn. I'm not supposed to be here—I'm not part of their community, but just passing through, using the post office or dry cleaner. I have become a stranger in their village. An exile.

My conversations come largely on the telephone now, with other writers, jazz and literary critics, and documentary filmmakers.

Many of them are white, some black or Jewish, and a few

Asian Americans. Another few come from abroad. They are of wider acquaintanceship. The phone chatter lasts me for a while—I laugh and get good stories, find out about new things to read and listen to, hear the latest in their lives, and gossip about publishing—but it isn't enough. I still get restless.

These days, to supplement this tricky, exilic kind of life, I've started making regular trips to Los Angeles. Sometimes I go on invitations to speak to students at UCLA or out in Claremont, to address a museum club and bookstore audiences in Pasadena and North Hollywood. Just as often, though, I make my own arrangements so I can stroll along the Third Street Promenade, cruise the 405 freeway and Santa Monica Boulevard, eat barbecue ("You don't need no teef to eat my beef!") and Chinese takeout, trying to reenter, as an adult, the world I grew up in.

This past winter I was on my way to Riverside, riding a shuttle from the Ontario airport. I was alone in the van with the driver, a young, streetwise guy who needed a haircut. He kept tucking and retucking his brown hair behind his ears, while the wind whipping in from the open driver's-side window repeatedly undid his work. He said that he was going to community college at night, taking courses in criminology. He was trying to prepare himself for work in law enforcement or as a prison guard. His name, he told me, was Presco Montoya.

"Presco?" I said.

"Pretty interesting name, huh?" he answered.

"Yeah," I said. "But I've heard it before. I used to know a Filipino cabdriver named Presco."

"You got it," he said. "Presco's short for Precioso—you know, Precious One. My mother's Filipina from Manila—she's romantic to the bone. My father's Chicano and tough, *pero*. They met overseas when he was in the military. They come home then, had me, and I grew up in El Monte."

I was liking anything he said by then because of the music in his voice, the way he formed his sentences, the torque and torsion of his speech. It had the city in it and a touch of some kind of twang I guessed might be from relatives who came from "the Valley"—which meant the San Joaquin Valley in my old circles. I told him I knew El Monte, that I used to go to dances there at the Legion Stadium when I was a teenager.

195

"Oh, yeah," he said, glancing up to the rearview mirror. He wanted a better look at my face, I guess. "You know, my uncle used to hang out there back in the sixties a lot, *vato.*"

He was letting his voice catch even more of a lilt.

"You know Rosie, of Rosie and the Originals?" he asked, looking in the rearview again, searching my eyes for a reaction. "Sure, I know them," I said, laughing softly. "Ahh, let me see . . ."

"Well," he said, "she used to come over to our house a lot when I was a kid."

I was impressed. I thought back to some oldies I'd slow-danced to in the sixties.

"'Angel Baby,'" I said, selecting the right tune from my memory.

"She used to go out with my uncle, you know?" Presco said. "I remember they would *lean* against the door of the pickup."

And the way he said that—slowing his speech way down, *decelerando*, shifting his hands on the wheel, scrunching up his face and his shoulders—made me laugh. I saw his uncle leaning a foxy lip-glossed Rosie up against the Turtle Waxed cherry red door of a citified pickup chopped low for cruising. She wore a sparkling sequined dress, and he was planting some deep, love-searching kiss down her throat, his rough hands riding up on her nyloned, barrio-soul-singer's leg. It was the L.A. version of a Cinzano poster, a kind of family photograph from the old days, and I got it simply by passing the time with the limo driver.

In L.A., whether I'm walking up the ramps and through the turnstiles in Dodger Stadium or ordering chow fun at the Far East Café in Little Tokyo, I feel a little grateful, even excited, to be reinhabiting uncelebrated zones of the familiar.

A Japanese American friend might pick me up at my hotel, pulling up to the curb by the lobby in a Lexus the color of silver fox. We'll drive over to Sawtelle on the West Side, stroll through the downscale streets where the community nurseries and Nisei import shops used to be in the fifties, and then find a place where we can order a nouvelle-sushi lunch. We'll talk about my trying a screenplay, doing some work that will be seen by millions. Distracted, I'll notice that the waitress looks like the sitcom Morticia Addams, except that what I thought were the cutout black sleeves of her dress are really dark, spidery tattoos covering her arms. Jiving with her, I find out her name is Sachiko, that she's the daughter of a community activist I used to know. It's a frail, almost absurd connection, but a connection nonetheless.

And inevitably, there will be someone—maybe a guy named Sol, short for Soldofsky, who went to Uni High—who tells me some intricate, speech-syncopated story about his ex-girlfriend Vivian-from-the-Valley, who, once a publicist for Tom Snyder, is now housewife to Sol's schlemiel cousin Stephen-from-Scarsdale, big deal, and they're rich as thieves, don't work for it, have a house in Topanga, buy their groceries at Bristol Farms, Nieman-Marcus-for-tomatoes, markup crazy.

It's not solely the style of the telling that does it for me, but Sol will wave a hand in a concomitant gesture I'll recognize as the Jewish sign of a sentimental love of place from the Lower East Side, itself evocative of my own infinite memories, then lean, some lazy, old-fashioned way, up against the outer brick wall of what used to be the Lighthouse jazz club out near the Hermosa Beach pier, and I'll be *home* suddenly, feeling the fog, funky-chicken in from slow offshore breakers I can't see but hear, like a good pulse running in my blood. I'll turn and smile to my companion then, take a drag from the cigar I got at the beachside stand, invoke the night in 1968 when I was busted at the Old Burbage Theater for watching a performance of Michael McClure's play *The Beard*, and walk up the strand with him, feeling puffs of wind fill up my sports-coat pockets like handfuls of spiritual change.

In L.A., moments like these occur for me all the time now. I seem to need their humble affirmations in order to survive. My sons, sweet innocents in their unpitiable cloisters of sameness and comfort, need to know these things, too. They need to know that diversity is not danger. I need to bring them into this brave new world.

America Singing

An Address to the Newly Arrived Peoples

Maybe you've seen the sign
On old Sepulveda. *Tai Song,*
Cantonese Cuisine, on your way
to or from the L.A. Airport.
    —Greg Pape

I've never been in Peking, or in the Summer Palace,
nor stood on the Great Stone Boat to watch
the rain begin on Kuen Ming Lake, the picnickers
running away in the grass.
But I love to hear it sung . . .
    —Li-Young Lee

I hear America singing, the varied carols I hear . . .
    —Walt Whitman

I am fascinated and thrilled that there has been such a surge of
new immigration from across the Pacific these past few years.
That, as a country, we are again in the process of being renewed
and reformed by the new Americans from Asia and elsewhere.
These newly arrived peoples, I know, come not so much from
Japan and Okinawa and Guangdong, as did the ancestors of we
third and fourth-generation Asian Americans, but rather they
are now coming, in increasing numbers, from Taiwan, Hong
Kong, Korea, Southeast Asia, Tonga, Fiji, Sāmoa, the Caribbe-
an, Central America, and the Philippines. Their presence has
charged our society with energy and change.

When I visit California now, and walk about in the resurgent
downtowns of San Jose and Santa Ana, I pass Vietnamese mar-

kets, Korean grocery stores, and restaurants for every kind of Pacific/Asian cuisine. When I was teaching at the University of Houston in 1988, I did most of my shopping in a huge super-supermarket run by Chinese for almost every Asian ethnicity—there was a Korean section, a section for Japanese foods (*nappa* cabbage, *daikon, kamaboko* fish cakes and *Kal-Pis* in the coolers), racks and racks of Chinese condiments like chili oil and oyster and plum sauces. I saw what I've always loved seeing—bins full of bean threads, bags of sesame seeds in various grades, cello-phaned flats of dried seaweed, cans of black beans and bamboo shoots, fifty-pound bags of rice. The smells were gorgeous. The market was in its own little complex of shops—a big parking lot ringed with little storefronts for a travel agency, an optom-etrist, a records and tapes store, a bookstore, a coffee and *dim sum* shop, a casual restaurant, and a movie theater that showed *chop-sockie* Saturday matinees, mildly lurid *cheongsam* romances weekend nights, and serials all week long.

I was taken there by one of my master's students, Edmund Chang, a graduate of Tufts in Boston, who was born in Taiwan, had grown up in Malta and Libya, went to high school in New Jersey, and had just become an American citizen the year before. He wanted to show me where to buy rice. We went with my small sons, themselves half-Asian, who loved the sweet rice candies, but wrinkled their noses at the carded, yellow circles of sliced, seal-wrapped octopus hanging on hooks near the check stand. And me—I loved the goddamn place. I loved the feeling of the throng of new peoples swirling around me. I loved the feeling that I was in a vortex of cultures, a new republic of exchange—the thrilled, New Americans around me. I heard a new chorus—it was America singing.

Before leaving Houston in 1989, I decided to get my car de-tailed. I didn't know if I was going to sell it or drive it to the West Coast where I was to take a new job. I took it to a detail shop I'd noticed while driving by one day. The guy there was a young hot-shot, a sassy white dude who could do everything—I knew it and he knew I knew it. I liked him. He had Benzes, Beamers, even a Maserati in his shop. There was a Volvo being vacuumed and shined up when I drove in. He gave me a guarantee and a good price. This was the place to get the job done right, I thought.

We made the deal and I handed him my keys. He leaned out of the little waiting room and yelled over to one of his employees inside the garage, who was busy shammying down a slick, black Riviera. "Juan-Oh!" he said, an inside joke between the two of them. Juan was a handsome, Native American-looking guy with thick, crow-black hair who was to drive me home in the shop car. He and I climbed into a Jeep Cherokee, freshly shined and, inside, its plastic wiped down with Armor All. We rode together in silence for a while, then, when I'd stood about as much of it as I could, I struck up a conversation.

"Where are you from?" I asked. His hair was jet-black, his skin rich and brown like stained Hawaiian *koa* wood. He held himself stiffly, and shifted gears with precision. He had the posture and build of a Navajo, I thought.

"El Salvador," he said, and turned his face to show me his grin.

"Oh," I said, surprised. In an instant, I felt annoyed with myself for being nosy. But I was curious, too. "Are you here to save your life?" I said.

"Yes, mine and my mother's, my wife's, my children's. We all come." There was silence again as we moved through traffic into the little university village near where I lived. I wanted to give him something.

"Do you know the phrase," I said, "El pueblo unído, jamás será vencido?" I learned it from my Chilean friends who had fled the murders after the coup of General Pinochet. It means, *The people, united, will never be defeated,* and was a slogan used to rally the various splinter groups of the Latin-American Left into united coalitions. Hundreds of thousands chanted this as they marched in demonstrations through the streets of Santiago in support of the democracy of Salvador Allende, the doctor and Socialist who was the elected president of Chile and who was deposed and murdered by his own military and, it is frequently said, with assistance from our CIA.

This Salvadoran man next to me turned and grinned again. "Yes, sir. I know this saying. It is full of heart. We in El Salvador say it too, though we die for it."

What unsettled me was his modesty, his resolve. Riding

through Houston in that car, we were both humbled by the histories we carried and invoked.

Some folks—a lot of white Americans who fear people like us, who fear the oncoming change as weak, inner-reef swimmers fear the largest swells at sea beyond the reef—look to our renewed cities with anger and pessimism, consider them now as *terra incognita*, lands where monsters dwell and where they are no longer safe or welcome. Many of the people I talk with in so-called educated circles feel that the inner cities, the ghettoes, are a demilitarized zone to them, an unknown, an X or Mysterious Island where others belong but not them, not the real Americans.

I remember a time—it was some years ago in '82 or so—I invited another poet out to lunch. He was older than me by a generation or so, a teacher of mine in a way, one who was part of the sixties' shift away from formal verse toward freer, more popularly accessible forms. I revered him a little and wanted to be his friend. He'd just moved to the suburbs east of Los Angeles, had a new job teaching at a private college there, and, as one who had grown up very eastern in Philadelphia, was missing cities and their splendors. I called him up and offered to show him L.A.'s Chinatown, take him for a *dim sum* at the Jade Gardens, my current favorite, and then to an afternoon movie downtown. We made the date and met at some designated corner of the city that weekend.

Dim sum started out fine. He marveled at the variety, at the tastes, at the throng of Asians all around us at round tables, the dozen or so carts like street vendors making their way around the huge upstairs hall of the restaurant. He said, "Oh, this is wonderful. Oh, this is better than Philly. Oh, how has the world kept this secret from me?" He went on to tell me about how he had met Ezra Pound, the great and politically strange poet of High Modernism. He told me about the revolution against formal metrics during the sixties and the wave of interest in open forms, primitive and international poetries, and social justice. He might have joined the black and white Freedom Riders who rode together on the buses to integrate the South, but he was too young then, he said.

But there were things about him that were enormously troubling. At the same time as I enjoyed his stories of his apprenticeship in the afterglow of Modernism, the generous accounts of his time scuffling up the literary ladder and finding his rung on it, I was disturbed by his other anecdotes, his ample scorn for other poets of his generation, and his complaints. He talked incessantly about a rival, another poet he'd once been close to, but with whom he'd had a severe falling out. He spent an entire course of *dim sum* bashing the other man's reputation and debunking his political theories, ridiculing his rival's lack of skill at "true" poetry—that which was metric and lovely and free of politics. As an ephebe in the art it was hard for me to listen; both men were genuine heroes to me. He then recanted much of his own work at midcareer, work done during the sixties when the two poets had been friends, calling his own poetry of that time— the poetry that I admired so much and had inspired me to seek him out—"sentimental, misguided, and stupid—*another man's poems.*" I poured tea for him in a small porcelain cup decorated with dragons, and he leaned toward me and said, "I didn't know what I was doing. I was on dope all the time and chasing girls and nirvana. I thought life was a circus and I wasn't serious."

We paid the check—a small amount, five dollars each—and rode a bus to a downtown theater: the old Orpheum, a once-lavish Fox palace gone the route of decay and semiabandonment. Yet it was open, showing a Richard Pryor comedy for the four o'clock matinee. We went. My friend marveled at the ornate appointments and plush chairs inside. He reminisced about his childhood in Philly. He laughed uproariously at the jokes, the sight gags, the crazy, convoluted plot that ended in a long chase scene. I relaxed and hoped the bitterness in him had been dispersed by our good time. We left the place euphoric and, junior that I was, I was pleased that I'd pleased him.

Outside, the city had turned dark. The sidewalks, moderately trafficked when we entered, were now thronged with Friday-night cruisers, crowds of the poor and hustling. Buses and dirty cars jammed the streets. We heard rap music from a huge stereo boom box a passerby shouldered like a cargo sack as he sauntered before us. Like the calliope music of a carousel that thrashes tide-like together with a Ferris wheel's countersongs and squeals from its riders, we heard disco pouring from the electronics store next door mingling with the car horns of traffic noise and hubbub from the passing crowd. A hawker in a red tuxedo and frilly dress shirt announced in Spanish that a ticket dance was fixing to start in the basement room below the movie theater. The New Americans surrounded us—Jamaicans in shiny polyester disco shirts, Cubanos and Puerto Ricans, Salvadorans, blacks from Watts and Compton and Inglewood, Chicanos from Whittier and East L.A. They were a processional of *penitentes*. The feeling was grand and powerful and strong. I felt the beat and wanted to dance.

My friend was terrified. He panicked, running out to the street and hailing down a bus, making it stop, banging on the pneumatic door until the driver hissed it open to let him in. He stared blankly for a moment and then recoiled at all the Asian, black, and Hispanic passengers' faces. He fell backwards from the bus and fled back to me, shouting. He pushed past me and ran for the street corner, where he may have seen a taxi cruise by.

I let him go. He had refuted all that I had loved about him. I recognized, finally, that he suffered from that Lethe-like, irrational wish—in poetry and in his concept of civilization—for an unblemished purity that can only be accomplished in death, that lavish extinguishment of desire and differences. There was in him a tremendous fear that may have begun, innocently, as mild cultural disdain, a kind of antipathy-budding-into-intolerance, which had eventually metastasized into a powerful Kurtz-like horror of those of us who come from struggle in the Heart of Darkness and want to help shape and belong to the New America. The general term is racism. And it grows strangely.

I remember one of my professors in graduate school—a place I still refer to as "Apartheid Tech"—sidling up to me at an afternoon reception and jostling me in a friendly way. I turned and he was beaming a little, clearly drunk from sampling the ample supply of reception chardonnay (though we were a state school there was always money for such things). "Hey Hahngo," he said, punching my shoulder, chummily macho. The happy people in the room around were oblivious, abuzz with their excited chatter, our mentors in sensible shoes and tweeds mixing with graduate students. I overheard someone pontificating on the lyrics to John Lennon's tunes, comparing them to Edmund Spencer's *Amoretti*.

"Hey Hahngo," the professor said again. "I hear you've got an interest in *Gook* lit." I felt the skin on my face freeze. I was stunned. I couldn't tell what he meant. "You know, that *minority* stuff," he continued. "I'm glad there's finally someone around here to cover it," he gestured with his plastic wineglass to the universe, "to fend off the Mongol hordes." He clapped me on the shoulder, turned away and ambled over to the tray of cheeses and grapes. The room with its plate glass windows opening to a view of California eucalyptus and blooming jacarandas gyred around me as if my place in it were the mirrors of a circus carousel. I was fixed to the earth, speechless. And sickened.

I look upon the newly arrived peoples—Hispanics, Afro-Caribbeans, Asians and Pacific Islanders, refugees and refuseniks from Europe—our new inhabitants of the inner cities, a new middle class renovating and swelling the suburban satellites around our cities, our new workers in the farm belts—with great hope and expectation. I know they are what my father was when he arrived in Los Angeles from Hawai'i thirty years ago. I know they are what my great-grandfathers were when they arrived, tanned and thinned by seasickness and lousy food, crossing over the long gangplank of the Immigration Station at Honolulu Bay over a hundred years ago. My grandfathers were the immigrant poor who were rich in hope and expectation. They would give their bodies and their spirits to make a place for their children in this new land. They would give us their singing, a small legacy of pain and sacrifice, and they would give us some of their courage.

I rode from the Upper East Side of Manhattan once, leaving early for a plane back to Hawai'i or Houston or Missouri or wherever it was I was teaching or fleeing from teaching that year. My driver, a guy I simply hailed down as I stood on the street corner in front of my hotel that morning, turned out to be an elderly man from Greece. Other times the man was from Russia or Jamaica or Korea or Romania. They each had a story. I glanced down at the identification shield hanging down from the visor over the passenger's seat in front, and I noticed his was a long, lavish name like Popaladopolous. "Mr. Popaladopolous," I began, "I am guessing you are Greek. Can you guess where I am from?" It is one of my favorite games when I travel. The night clerk from Poland stationed at the front desk of my hotel guessed Singapore. The Egyptian cardiac surgeon who wanted to buy my freshly detailed car in Houston guessed China or Taiwan.

"You are right," my Greek driver said, "But you have the advantage over me—you know my name."

"I am Hohngo," I said, giving it the Japanese pronunciation, as I would back home in Hawai'i. On the mainland, in "America," I give in and pronounce in "Hahngo," attuning myself to the dominant accent that calls my Senator Daniel Inouye, officially, "Inui."

"Oh," Popaladopolous said, "you are a complicated man. You are an American from California or Los Angeles, and you are Oriental. Your father maybe came from Japan?"

"Very good," I said. "You are almost perfectly right. I am from Hawai'i, and yes, my great-grandfather came from Japan."

The traffic was intense. We ran into the infamous Manhattan gridlock as we headed toward the East River and one of the bridges. I asked what he was doing in America. He told me he had been an attorney in Greece, a prominent man of his city, with a family—a wife and several daughters. Then the Colonels took over. "Do you know the Colonels?" he asked me.

I knew there had been the terrible conflict between the different factions in Greece. The Costa-Gavras film *Z* is about that. The books *When a Tree Sings* and *Eleni* by my friends Stratis Haviaras and Nicholas Gage tell opposite sides of a tough story. I remembered the headlines about Greece when I was a teenager in Los Angeles, the exile of the king, the military dictatorship, and the protest of the oppression by film star Melina Mercouri. I thought of the poet Yannis Ritsos and how he had lived so long in detention and internal exile in a prison on an island that was a concentration camp for members of the Left. "Yes," I said, "I know the Colonels."

"I was an attorney in Greece, in Athens—a dirty but beautiful city. I was a leader and supported the wrong side. I came to America. I brought my family. My daughter, she is grown now, and she is next week taking the New York bar examination. She will be a lawyer as well. Here, let me show you. Come with me."

Popaladopolous jumped out of the taxi and motioned for

me to do the same. The traffic was still locked around us. He went to the back and lifted the battered trunk lid. There were clothes, books, a loose-leaf binder. He grabbed a small parcel. Inside were photographs and a certificate.

"See?" he said, pointing and holding up a snapshot. "Here is my daughter in red and my nieces and myself in back." I saw buxom young women in party dresses and heavy makeup and Mr. Popaladopolous in a gray suit standing behind them. "This is her graduation from Hofstra School of Law. We take her to the restaurant of my son-in-law." He flipped through more photographs— his house in Queens, his old house in Athens, snaps of an island holiday in Eretria many years ago—and, finally, he held up the certificate I'd noticed, wrapped in yellowing plastic.

"To be an attorney," he said, "this is my diploma from Greece." For an instant, he held it up over our heads like a chalice and then handed it to me. "So, you see," he said, "I am telling truth to you." I saw it was smallish, only 5" x 7" or so, but there were seals and signatures on it. I nodded yes, I believed him. "But why do you not practice here?" I asked, though I knew the answer. It was ritual. "This is not possible," he said brusquely. He could not return to law school, to study for the bar, to begin again as a clerk, then associate, and so on. "I must work for my family, feed them, send my daughter to school. Give them my future. I drive cab, make money. The house in Queens. We are Americans now. Greece is the past. I am lonely for it, but here I live."

The traffic loosened around us. We got back in his cab and sped away to La Guardia, feeling our common resolve.

Some years ago, on leave from Missouri, I went to Los Angeles to do some poetry readings. It was winter, January in Southern California, and the great beauty of the place was in the snow-lined ridges of the Angeles Crest and the San Gabriel Mountains, a stunning natural backdrop to the city that swarmed around us in its infinite patterns of distraction. You could be driving from the south up the Harbor Freeway and the mountains would be constantly before you, blue behemoths splashed and lichened with snow. This time of year, the air was clear as summer in the Arctic, and visibility stretched from the pier at Long Beach to the Hale Telescope at the Cal Tech Observatory on the ridgeline above the city.

One morning I gave a reading to a teenage audience at Alhambra High School, a place just east of Pasadena tucked in one of the canyon valleys against the San Gabriels. I drove up from the south where I was staying and parked my rented car under an enormous palm tree next to a warehouse a few blocks from the school. I like Alhambra. It was an older section of the metropolis, built up during the forties and fifties and the aircraft boom; the scale and vintage of the streets and buildings seemed to come straight out of a Raymond Chandler novel. I noticed small custom garages, a coin shop, bakeries, a few restaurants and diners, and one place with that classic extravagance of neon, stainless steel, asphalt, and glass that could only mean a drive-in.

The day's event was sponsored by California State University Los Angeles, an idea thought up by Carl Selkin, director of their Poetry Center and my host. This was to be part of an outreach program by the university to the communities nearby, gone largely "ethnic." It was an experiment run as part of the celebration commemorating Dr. Martin Luther King's birthday. At Cal State L.A. the day before, Selkin had explained that the poet on their faculty had not been interested in doing this, had found it impossible to reach an audience he deemed "largely illiterate." But the high school English teachers—many of them graduates of CSU's excellent education program—were thrilled with the idea. Two of them had studied with Zbigniew Herbert, the great postwar Polish poet who had once taught at Cal State L.A. in the sixties. They wanted me to come, so I agreed.

I was put in a large science classroom where I sat in front of a huge desk with a sink on one end and a kind of projector that looked like a clunky, off-scale microscope on the other. The teachers told me I would read to an assembly made up largely of Asians and whites—about a hundred students, most of them juniors and seniors. The Asians were a mixture of Chinese and Southeast Asians, they told me, some of them Vietnamese, some Cambodians, a lot of them from Hong Kong as well. Some four or five English classes were put together to make up the audience, and the students trooped in and took their seats, the whites giggling and self-conscious, the Asians largely silent.

I read my poems about the inner city and my poems about

Hawai'i, about my leaving there as a child, returning to it many years later as an adult, a poet, and seeking out the old places—the plantation lands, the sugar mills, the canefield and grave-yard where I might have played as a child, the rough seashore that was like kin. I read a long poem about walking through the old Japanese cemetery in Kahuku on the plantation, told them how it was placed on a promontory overlooking the sea on a sandy point jutting into the ocean. I told them how we Japanese and Filipinos and Chinese put our cemeteries there because it was the land given to us by the growers who needed the good land, the land that was arable, for growing the sugar cane and pineapple. But what we didn't know, what the growers didn't know, was that the sea would come and take our dead from us then, in the periodic raids of rips and tidal waves from a swelling ocean. The Hawaiians knew this. They took the bones of their dead to the high ground, up to the caves on the cliffs and the rock mounds on the rainy plateau above the shelves of land, be-tween the sea and the windward mountains. But we immigrants, we newly arrived laborers, placed generation after generation in the sand by the sea.

A *tsunami* came in 1946 and took over half of our dead in one night. "Bones and tombstones / up and down the beach," my poem said. I told them of walking over the patchy carpeting of temple moss "yellowing in the saline earth," the stinging sand clouds kicked up by the tough, onshore wind. I recalled a story of a murder committed out of outrage and shame—it was an act of victimage committed *within* the community—and paid hom-age to it as part of my past. It was to the journey I paid homage, the quest and travail of it from an Asian past to our American present. And it was to its remembrance—as shame and pride—that the poem was dedicated.

When I was finished, I looked up. In the back row was a Chi-nese girl, or maybe she was Vietnamese, dressed in a plain white school shirt and dark woolen skirt. Her hair was long and hung in two thick braids against her ears and jaw. Her eyes were shin-ing. She wept, staring at me as if I were a statue. I averted my eyes, glancing quickly across the row and throughout the assem-bly, and saw others weeping too, wiping their faces. Some were embarrassed and gazed down at the floor or at their shoes. A few teachers nodded. I don't remember anyone smiling. Nothing like it had ever happened to me before. There was a heaviness in the room, a momentary silence. I was surprised and a little unsettled by it.

The assembly broke up, a teacher standing and thanking everyone, gesturing toward me and calling for more applause. Then the classes began filing out, and an Asian girl came up to me and asked me to sign her Pee-Chee. Another had me sign a napkin. A few more had xeroxes of my poems. I signed them all. A boy with acne and hair cut close to his temples but thick with pomade at the top—it was a style then coming into fashion with urban rappers—asked if I'd be reading for "adults" anytime that week. He wanted his parents to hear me, too. I phlumphered something about the Pacific-Asian Museum that Saturday.

I had lunch with the teachers. They took me to the cafeteria, and we sat at the long bench tables I remembered from my public school days. Over the fish sticks and tapioca pudding, we talked poetry and the new Asian students. A youngish man dressed in brown tweeds then spoke. He had a light brown beard, neatly trimmed.

"I've never seen them respond like that," he said. "Never seen them act so openly, show emotion like that before. You really connected."

I was learning something, something new and strong. These children with so much passion, so much raw affection, were teaching me that I had an audience, that my experience and sensibility spoke for their experiences, that I could address a world of others like myself, of Asians newly arrived, of peoples wanting to make America their place too. Up until then, I'd pretty much felt embattled as an artist and took it as part of my identity. I saw myself as an individual presence up against cultural ignorance or mild hostility, particularly because my subject—the history of Japanese in America—was something I thought few cared to hear about. Except for some wonderful exceptions, and most of these among my fellow poets, I'd felt that, even if I were allowed a place in academe or the literary world, it would be on sufferance; no one was *intrinsically* interested in my obsessions, my passions. I thought of America as an establishment apart from me. But after that assembly beside the

Los Angeles mountains, signing the Pee-Chees and napkins and xeroxes those teenage students had of my poems, I sensed that I was beginning to belong to something, to join a throng of voices in need of their own singing.

When Walt Whitman, the great American poet of the nineteenth century, wrote his poems of robust American optimism, full of the democratic spirit and lust for challenges and union jobs, he shouted, "I Hear American Singing!," and announced a theme that characterized more than a century of our history. Well, I look upon all of us here, now, we, the renewed Americans, among the freshly arrived peoples with their boat trails of memories from across the oceans, and, I think, *I Hear America Singing* too.